Because Money Matters:

How to Find and Get

a Better Job

V. V. CAM

Disclaimer: The general information provided in this book may not apply to your specific situation. The information is accurate as of the publication date and it is subject to change. All links to websites, companies and service providers are provided for your convenience only. Please consult individual websites for current information regarding their practice, policies and pricing, etc.

The author is not a financial advisor, attorney, or accountant. Please consult with the appropriate personnel or agencies in your country for advice on finance, legal, and taxation matters.

CONTENTS

WHY DID I WRITE THIS BOOK?

I remember that summer morning, a couple of weeks before my 16th birthday when I went inside a small local bedding store. The owner didn't believe me when I said to her in broken English that I knew how to use a sewing machine and that I was looking for a job. She pointed to a nearby sewing machine, gave me two small pieces of fabric, and asked me to sew them together. Remembering everything my mother had taught me, I sat down nervously, closed my eyes, took a deep breath, and then did everything with that machine that my mother had shown me. You can't imagine how proud I felt as I came out of the shop with packages of pre-cut materials ready to be sewn. There I was, a little more than a year after walking out of a refugee camp, I had a job in my new country: sewing duvets on consignment!

Actually, my employment journey started when I was 13 working in an electronics factory in Hong Kong. Since I arrived in Canada, I have had many jobs, sometimes concurrently or at minimum rates. Some of the other jobs I had were: tax preparer, waitress, bartender, receptionist, office clerk, administration assistant, computer support/specialist/trainer, and real estate agent/broker. I've also held executive positions that plan and manage finances, human resources, and relationships. Currently, I manage information technology projects for a large organization, earning a six-figure salary with benefits and an exceptional pension plan.

In my 40 plus years in the workforce, I worked at each job long enough to be ready for a new experience. With each job, I learned different skills and a little more about myself. I used the tools outlined in this book to help me move from one position to another. Every new job has helped, prepared, and led me to a better one to keep me feeling worthy, happy, and fulfilled.

I want to inspire you to do the same. You can change the course of your career for the better.

I've had my fair share of interviews, both as an interviewee and as an interviewer. I want to share my knowledge and experiences to help you be strategic in your career. The tools provided in this book will teach you a methodical approach to finding, applying for, and landing a job. I will show you how to package your experience to increase your chance of getting your next job where you feel happy and valued.

In my previous book, *Because Money Matters: The 8 Principles to Build Your Wealth,* I shared the principles my mother gave me to build wealth and sustain financial success. In this book, I want to share the knowledge and experiences I've shared with my teenage daughter to help prepare her for her future career.

About this book

Landing a job offer involves more than picking the format for your résumé, deciding on what to include in your cover letter, and preparing for your interview. I will share tips and tools that will make you a striking and desirable candidate. More importantly, I will demystify the job-search process and give you a method you can use to increase your chance of landing the job you want, whether it is your first job or your dream job.

With practical real-world experience, I've developed this Competency-Aligned Skills & Traits (CAST) method that I used to continuously and successfully transition to better jobs. The method borrows the "plug-and-play" and "building blocks" concepts in computing. In plug-and-play, a user only needs to "plug" a device into a computer and it will start working or "play". This ability increases efficiency and standardization. Each step in the CAST process acts as a building block which can then be integrated as part of a versatile and dynamic system. The method also uses the "build once, use many" approach to simplify the job applying process by making each piece of information reusable rather than compiling information for every job you plan to apply. You build your CAST profile only once, keep it current, and then choose the different pieces for different jobs. The method is useful for any job seeker, especially for those who struggle in getting interviews or getting job offers and for those who often avoid applying for jobs because of the effort- and time-consuming process. You will be able to use the insight and knowledge you gain throughout your working life.

This book isn't about figuring out which career is right for you; it's about getting a job in the career you desire. It covers the traditional hiring process where an applicant applies for a position by sending his/her résumé and cover letter, gets interviewed, then gets a job offer. It is intended to be used as a workbook and for people seeking non-managerial office jobs even though it can be applied to other positions. Among many other things, you will learn:

- The three key concerns that every employer has and how to address them.

- How to align your qualifications with the 28 most-common core competencies that employers look for.

- How to assess your technical ability.

- How to turn your past experiences into impactful qualification statements.

- How to create convincing stories of your experiences that highlight your competencies.

- How to formulate your unique qualification statements and interview answers using fill-in-the-blank templates.

- How to incorporate keywords to create impressive and effective personal brand statements, résumés, and cover letters that emphasize your competencies.

- How to prepare for and use the ABC principles to handle interviews with ease, confidence, and without stress.

- Questions you should always ask and questions you should always avoid.

- How to deal effectively with any salary questions to preserve your negotiating power.

- How to properly accept or decline a job offer.

Plus, you'll also gain free online access to all templates, checklists, and other bonus materials to give you everything you need to help you through each step.

Of course, reading any book will not guarantee you a job, but I hope reading this book will show you the ways to increase your chance of getting the job you qualify for and make your job searching journey less overwhelming. You will be proud of your accomplishments, encouraged by the possibilities, and excited about the prospects.

Let us do this together.

1. TAKING STOCK

There are many concepts and definitions of what a perfect job should look like. For some, it could be the job with the shortest commute, for others the perfect job might have the highest pay.

If you don't know exactly what your perfect job looks like, use the following self-assessment to determine what you value most. This assessment helps you focus on jobs that match your preferences. This is not about chasing an unrealistic dream job, but about setting achievable goals that leave you feeling happy and fulfilled.

1.1   Self-Assessment: What do I want in a job?

For each statement in column A (and any additional statements you may add):

1. Place a check mark in Column B if you get that in your current job. If you don't currently have a job, skip this step.

2. Place a check mark in column C if that is what you want in a job.

3. After all items are checked off, in column D, rank the items you've checked off in Column C in the order of importance. For example, 1 for the most important, 2 for the next important, and so forth.

(A) A job...	(B) Have	(C) Want	(D) Rank
that pays me fairly according to my ability.			
that has the benefits (including time off) that I need.			
that is close to my home.			

(A) A job...	(B) Have	(C) Want	(D) Rank
that is not stressful.			
that has good and safe working conditions.			
that allows me to have more responsibility and grow.			
where my employer and colleagues respect me.			
that allows me to have more challenging and exciting work.			
where I get the support I need.			
where I am treated fairly.			
that gives me the status and/or title I want.			
that gives me fewer responsibilities.			
where I feel valued and appreciated.			
that gives me the level of satisfaction I want.			

(A) A job...	(B) Have	(C) Want	(D) Rank
that gives me purpose.			
where I feel physically and mentally safe.			
with a company where everyone is committed to doing quality work.			
that gives me the work-life balance I need.			
with a bigger (or smaller) organization.			
that gives me the long-term prospects I want.			
that allows me to work flexible hours.			
that allows me to telework.			
with an ethical company.			
with an organization whose culture I like.			
that gives me more learning opportunities.			
that allows me to fully use my skills and experiences.			

(A) A job...	(B) Have	(C) Want	(D) Rank
that gives me more opportunities for advancement.			
that provides the security and stability I need.			
that gives me clear direction and expectation.			
that gives me the proper tools I need to do my work.			
with an organization that has effective leadership.			
where I have good relationships with my manager and colleagues.			
where the organization offers programs such as private medical services, professional training, and private career coaching.			
where it is accessible.			

(A) A job...	(B) Have	(C) Want	(D) Rank
where the organization is pet-friendly.			
that adds value to our world.			
that keeps me motivated by its nature.			
where I enjoy working with the people.			
where the employer trusts me.			
where the organization values family.			
that fits my personality.			
where the organization's values align with mine.			

Looking at your self-assessment, if you currently don't have a job, you now know what to look for in one. Start with section 1.4 to help you prepare for it.

If you are currently working, chances are slim that you have everything you want in your current job or that your circumstances will remain the same over time. Redo the self-assessment when needed and at any time you wonder whether you should look for a new job, use the following self-assessment to help with that question.

1.2   Self-Assessment: When should I look for a new job?

Check all the statements below that apply to your situation.

☐ I am bored all the time and no longer challenged in my position. I can do my duties well without much effort. I have tried to communicate with management but not much has changed. I frequently check the time at work and spend most of my workday on the Internet, playing games, or doing non-work tasks.

☐ I feel that I am not reaching my full potential. I feel stuck in a position that doesn't allow me to use my skills or learn new ones in the past few months.

☐ I feel my organization doesn't offer opportunities for growth and advancement. I don't feel a sense of usefulness, self-confidence, or accomplishment.

☐ I feel the organization's goals and my personal goals don't match up. For example, my job doesn't offer the work-life balance or advancement I'd like.

☐ I feel like I constantly fight losing battles.

☐ I feel my life is in a chronic state of stress and exhaustion. My performance is affected by my lack of energy and enthusiasm.

☐ I feel my manager doesn't show appreciation and always expects more from me even though I exceed in my performance.

☐ I've often been asked to take on tasks without adequate guidance or ownership. These extra tasks demand long hours, cause frustration and lack of motivation.

☐ I don't feel comfortable laughing, showing excitement, or celebrating at work.

☐ I feel I must watch what I say. I often must avoid saying what I think and I worry about how my comments would be interpreted.

☐ I get overwhelmed by the smallest things. I get upset and stressed out. I am no longer able to handle even little setbacks.

☐ I feel my organization doesn't care about my engagement.

☐ I don't make enough to pay my bills. My organization offers infrequent and small raises.

☐ I feel my pay isn't consistent with my workload. My organization makes me feel like they are doing me a favour by paying me.

☐ There are several indications and talks about downsizing, acquisitions, or mergers.

☐ I am not proud to discuss my workplace with my friends.

☐ I am not excited about the work I'll be doing or the people I'll work with.

☐ I can't picture where I'll most likely be in the organization in a year.

☐ I believe my manager or company engage in unethical activities and they may expect me to partake.

- ☐ I have an unbearable manager whose attitude doesn't just affect my time at work but also affects other important aspects of my life.

- ☐ I believe the poor working situation affects my health. I start to experience stress symptoms like heartburn and nausea.

- ☐ I long for the weekends when I feel like I've been freed.

- ☐ I found myself wishing to win the lottery just so I don't ever have to go back to my job.

- ☐ I know I could get better compensation, recognition, or other benefits elsewhere for what I do.

- ☐ I have a better job offer or I have started my business and I am ready to move on.

- ☐ I feel it is the right thing to look for a new job.

- ☐ I call in sick on a semi-regular basis just so I don't have to face work.

- ☐ I feel I am being taken advantage of.

☐ I don't feel my workplace or company culture is ideal. My manager isn't interested in getting to know me and what's going on in my personal life.

☐ My manager does not have the necessary leadership skills. I am frustrated that he/she does not give proper feedback or coaching and does not set clear expectations.

☐ Despite how hard I have worked or how well I am doing at my job, I will not be promoted to a higher paying and more demanding position.

☐ I don't feel safe.

☐ I get harassed, bullied, or discriminated.

☐ My organization practises unfair promotion. I lost my chance to someone less qualified and less capable for a position that I wanted.

☐ I've made extra effort and worked more hours when needed but I didn't get the bonuses or benefits that were promised.

If you've checked off any items from the list, they are signs or reasons that you may want to consider looking for a better job.

1.3   Considerations before changing career

Before deciding to change jobs, also ask yourself the following questions to decide if this is the right time to change your career.

- Why do I want to change?

- Am I ready for change?

- What will happen to my current networks and relationships?

- Am I open to new ideas and new ways of doing things?

- Will I need and am I able to learn new tools and/or methodologies?

- Will I be comfortable in a new work culture or environment?

- How long will it take me to adapt to a new environment?

- How will my life and family life be affected?

- Do I change jobs too often (for example, every job is held for less than six months)?

1.4   Skills, capabilities, and competencies

Before moving on, take stock of the skills that form the basis of your résumé. Understanding your hard skills and soft skills will prepare you for your next job.

Hard skills are the ability to do specific tasks. They are often based on technical knowledge or training. Hard skills might include reconciling accounts, writing sales copy, and designing websites. Speaking, writing, calculating, reading, programming are hard skills. Proficiency in a foreign language and typing speed are also examples of these skills. Often different jobs require different technical skills. Many technical skills require experience and some require extensive training to master.

Soft skills often referred to as "people skills" or "social skills" are abilities that relate to emotional intelligence. Soft skills are hard to define because they are often intangible. Such non-technical abilities can be difficult to categorize and measure. These include personal skills such as time management, innovative thinking, or decision making. Some soft skills are also linked to personal emotions or behaviours that enable someone to interact effectively and harmoniously with people such as the ability to work with, lead, or persuade others. Behaviours include ingrained traits (for example, introverts and extroverts) and acquired attributes (for example, motivation and enthusiasm).

1.4.1   The 3 CANS of competencies

While you are looking for a job that suits you, a prospective employer is hoping to find someone who can do the job well and be happy and proud doing it. The hiring manager would spell out the requirements with different words and ask questions in different ways to determine whether you can alleviate his/her three main concerns:

1. Can you <u>do</u> the job?

2. Can you <u>fit in</u>?

3. Can you <u>be trusted</u>?

Let's take a few moments to understand what the concerns are behind these three CAN questions.

1.4.1.1 Can you <u>do</u> the job?

This first question is for determining your qualifications and abilities. It is about your experience, education, and knowledge. It is also about your ability to produce consistent quality work. The hiring manager wants to know things like:

- Do you have the technical skills required?

- Do you have computer experience?

- How did you gain your abilities?

- Can you be creative?

- Can you follow directions?

- Can you plan, organize, and prioritize?

- Can you manage and meet deadlines?

- Can you think analytically, critically, and laterally?

- Can you troubleshoot and solve problems?

- Can you make sound decisions?

- Can you produce consistent results?

1.4.1.2 Can you <u>fit in</u>?

This question is for determining your interactions and awareness. It is about people, settings, and emotions. The hiring manager wants to know things like:

- Do you understand your role in the organization?

- How well do you fit under the organization's structure?

- Will your personality mix well with others who already work there?

- How do you work, contribute, and behave?

- How do you handle difficult people and stress?

- How aware are you of your own strengths and weaknesses?

- How do you feel about changes?

- Will you be satisfied with the job?

1.4.1.3 Can you **be trusted?**

This question is for determining your outlook and beliefs. It is about your traits and values. The hiring manager wants to know things like:

- Are you trustworthy, dependable, and flexible?

- Do your personal values align with those of the organization?

- How committed are you to the organization's ideals?

- Will you comply with the organization's procedures, directives, and policies?

- Will you protect the organization's assets and reputation?

- Will you stand up for your beliefs and convictions?

- Will you advocate for the organization?

- How confident or motivated are you?

- How positive is your attitude?

- Can you learn from criticism and mistakes?

- Will you take initiative?

- Will you do what it takes?

- Will you keep on learning and growing?

Imagine you are in a competition where someone who can fill three clearly-labelled empty cans with the most-needed ingredients wins. The contest would be easy because you just need to fill each can with the matching ingredients.

Looking for a job is also a competition. But during the hiring process, employers don't say they have concerns and they don't simply ask the three CAN questions. Instead, they give you a list of requirements and look for indicators of the necessary competencies that can address their concerns.

In section 1.4.2, you will learn a method that helps you identify competencies from your experiences, hard skills, and soft skills and how to use them to match the employer's requirements so that you get a better chance at winning. The remaining chapters of this book are organized around the three concerns every employer has. Now let's talk about competencies.

1.4.1.4 The competency wheel

Competencies are a group of skills, behaviours, and performance levels that employers use to determine your suitability for a particular role. Some competencies are found across all positions while some are found in specific industries or jobs.

The competency wheel below illustrates 28 of the most-common core competencies. They are divided into two categories: 12 job-specific (C1 to C12) and 16 standard competencies. The standard competencies are further divided into three groups: nine in soft skills or behaviours relating to activities (C13 to C21), four relating to interactions (C22 to C25), and three relating to personal characteristics (C26 to C28). The following table explains the competencies and while some job-specific competencies may not apply to your situation, the standard ones are required for most jobs.

COMPETENCIES

STANDARD COMPETENCIES · beliefs · education · experience · JOB-SPECIFIC COMPETENCIES · processes · quality · COMPETENCIES · research · systems · tools · skills · people · emotions

TRUST IN DO

TRAITS & VALUES

QUALIFICATIONS & ABILITIES

INTERACTIONS & AWARENESS

C27-Compliance
C26-Personal development
C1-Technical capability
C2-Equipment and program knowledge
C3-Customer relationship mgmnt
C4-Research
C5-Data analysis
C6-Identifying patterns or connections
C7-Policies
C8-Planning
C9-Business acumen
C10-Speaking and listening
C11-Writing
C12-Computer literacy
C13-Time management
C14-Analytical thinking
C15-Resourcefulness
C16-Communication
C17-Negotiation
C18-Persuasion
C19-Problem solving
C20-Decision making
C21-Commitment
C22-Interpersonal awareness
C23-Collaboration
C24-Handling pressure and stress
C25-Change management
C26-Resourcefulness
C27-Compliance and ethics

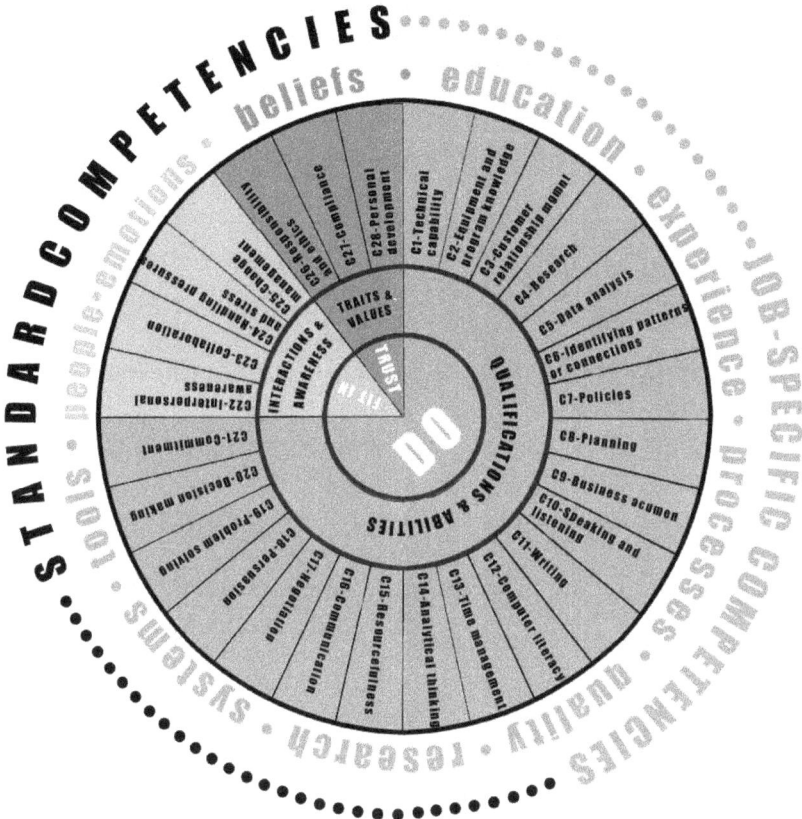

JOB SPECIFIC COMPETENCIES

C1	Technical capability
	Ability to demonstrate depth of knowledge and skills in a technical area.
C2	Equipment and program knowledge
	Ability to diagnose equipment or process issues.

C3	**Customer relationship management** Ability to adopt processes to provide positive interactions with customers, resolve issues, and handle complaints effectively in a timely manner.
C4	**Research** Ability to identify the information needed to clarify a situation, seek that information from appropriate sources, and use skillful questioning to draw out the information when others are reluctant to disclose it.
C5	**Data analysis** Experience in collecting and analyzing different data sets to obtain business insights.
C6	**Identifying patterns or connections** Ability to identify underlying issues and trends in complex situations, to locate inconsistencies between situations that are not obviously related, and to use inductive reasoning to form ideas about groups of events or situations.

C7	**Policies** Knowledge of why policies are important and how they link to business values and cultures.
C8	**Planning** Ability to identify trends and developments in advance, anticipate stumbling blocks, and developing contingency plans.
C9	**Business acumen** Ability to analyze the organization's competitive position by considering market and industry trends, existing and potential customers, and strengths and weaknesses compared to competitors. It also includes the ability to look for and seize profitable business opportunities and the willingness to take calculated risks to achieve business goals.
C10	**Speaking and listening** Ability to speak clearly and listen attentively.

C11	**Writing** Ability to structure ideas clearly and use concise, clear, appropriate language to convey them succinctly and effectively.
C12	**Computer literacy** Experience with relevant software packages and the ability to learn new systems quickly.

STANDARD COMPETENCIES

Activities	
Activities	
C13	**Time management** Ability to use resources effectively to achieve objectives or to prioritize workload to meet deadlines. It is the process of organizing and planning how to divide time between activities to increase efficiency and reduce stress.
C14	**Analytical thinking** Ability to break complex tasks into manageable segments and identify potential problems using a logical, systematic, sequential approach to find effective solutions. It is about taking a holistic, abstract, or theoretical perspective;

	anticipating the implications and consequences of situations; and taking appropriate action to be prepared for possible contingencies.
C15	**Resourcefulness** Ability to use existing resources or knowledge to devise new ways of working and to tackle unexpected challenges. It is about being open-minded about possibilities and using talents and resources to fulfill goals so that more can be done for less. It is not just for creating something new, but also for improving existing things.
C16	**Communication** Ability to use appropriate tools and languages to explain information clearly and concisely and to express emotions appropriately.
C17	**Negotiation** Ability to address key concerns and present mutually beneficial solutions intended to reach an understanding or agreement.

C18	**Persuasion** Ability to use audience-specific language and examples to present arguments to illustrate and support own positions in order to gain others' support.
C19	**Problem solving** Ability to identify and analyze the causes and effects of problems and to come up with appropriate solutions using logic, judgment, and data.
C20	**Decision making** Ability to prioritize different needs and analyze data and information to make considered decisions in a timely manner.
C21	**Commitment** Ability to produce high-quality work that meets or exceeds the organization's requirements and seek new ways to improve productivity.

	Interactions
C22	**Interpersonal awareness** Ability to recognize and regulate own emotions and behaviours and to recognize and respect others' emotions and perspectives.
C23	**Collaboration** Ability to build strong relationships through honest communication, active sharing, participation, and cooperation.
C24	**Handling pressures and stress** Ability to manage feelings or symptoms of stress and respond calmly to criticism.
C25	**Change management** Ability to embrace, support, and promote organizational change or to help others manage the emotional impact of change.

Personal Characteristics	
C26	**Responsibility and ethics** Ability to take responsibility for own actions and mistakes, respect values and confidential agreements, and demonstrate high standards of ethical conduct and behaviours consistent with the organization's policies.
C27	**Compliance** Ability to recognize and support the organization's structure, policies, and its value of diversity.
C28	**Personal development** Ability to take responsibility for one's own performance by setting clear goals and expectations, tracking progress against the goals, ensuring feedback, and addressing performance problems and issues promptly. It is also about personality and those drivers that influence thinking, feeling and behaviour.

As you can see, while a hiring manager is most interested in your competencies in doing the job well, he/she wants to know about competencies in human interactions and your personal values.

The hiring manager will likely focus the job advertisement and interview around those competencies that are most important and relevant. The candidate who can demonstrate as many competencies as possible has the best chance of getting the job.

Employers will likely assess your competencies through your résumé, your cover letter, and your interview. They are looking for consistency among them.

Résumés	Cover Letters	Interviews
C1-C21	C26-C28	C1-C28
What do you know and what did you do?	Who are you and what else can you tell me?	How did you do what you said you know or did?

From your side, you use your résumé to show your competencies. You use your cover letter to introduce yourself, to emphasize certain competencies, and to mention other important relevant details. You use an interview to tell how you did the things you mentioned in your résumé.

Now, let's use the CAST method to assess your present situation and create your CAST profile to see how it aligns.

1.4.2   The CAST method

CAST stands for Competency-Aligned Skills & Traits—a method I developed over the years to assess my competencies. I have used it successfully to get better job offers. The CAST method makes the job application process quicker and easier. It also increases the chances that your application will lead to a job offer.

Use the following six steps to create your CAST profile. From the profile you will be able to select the pieces you need to prepare effective résumés, cover letters, and interviews:

1. **Section 1.4.2.1 – Can I do the job?** – Uncover your abilities and qualifications competencies (C1 to C21) behind the tasks you do.

2. **Section 1.4.2.2 – Can I fit in?** – Uncover your interaction and awareness competencies (C22 to C25) behind the tasks you do.

3. **Section 1.4.2.3 – Can I be trusted?** – Create your trait and value statements (C26 to C28) to be used for preparing cover letters.

4. **Section 1.4.2.4** – Create your competency map from steps 1 to 3 above.

5. **Section 1.4.2.5** – Create your qualification statements from step 4 above to be used for preparing résumés.

6. **Section 1.4.2.6** – Create your CAR stories to be used for preparing interviews.

To start, download the "My CAST profile" worksheet from http://www.because.zone/join-us/bmm3-reg/ or create your own as we go along. The downloadable worksheet includes all the templates in sections 1.4.2 and 1.4.3.

1.4.2.1 Step 1: Can I do the job?

The 12 job-specific competencies (C1 to C12) are different for each job and each industry. You need to have the specific knowledge, experience, and ability to do the job you apply for. Use the self-assessment in section 1.4.2.1a as a guide to help you know which areas you need to improve. Section 1.4.2.1b suggests ways you can acquire new skills, improve existing skills, or gain relevant experience.

1.4.2.1a Self-Assessment: How well do I know the job?

Check all the statements below and any additional statements that apply to you or the job that you are applying for. You will need to work on all unchecked statements.

- ☐ I know what competencies are required for this job.

- ☐ I can rate my key competencies.

- ☐ I can describe how to do typical job-specific tasks and when, where, and why I need to do them.

- ☐ I know how much time should be spent on typical job-specific tasks.

- ☐ I know the job-specific procedures, processes, and policies.

- ☐ I can describe the steps in a job-specific process.

- ☐ I know which job-specific tools/systems I need and I know how to use them.

- ☐ I know how to assess and ensure delivery of high-quality work.

- ☐ I have the required education or certification for this job.

- ☐ I can describe what I do to maintain my job-specific education or certification.

☐ I know the definitions and terminologies appropriate for this job.

☐ I know the job-specific roles. For example, in this job I will be working with colleagues, managers, customers, business partners, stakeholders, etc.

☐ I know the job-specific functions and roles. For example, in this job, I will collaborate with colleagues, consult with managers, serve customers, communicate with business partners, engage stakeholders, etc.

☐ I can describe the necessary elements required for building successful relationships, projects, or systems such as providing customer service, building a team, and getting consensus.

☐ I know what I can, cannot, will, must, and may do in this job.

☐ I know the job-specific common and best practices.

☐ I know my job-specific strengths and weaknesses.

☐ I can recite my responsibilities in my most recent project/job.

☐ I have a good understanding of what I will be doing daily based on the description of the position.

☐ I can think of the challenges that this position may have and I have plans to overcome them.

1.4.2.1b Ways to learn

If you don't have some of the job-specific skills you need, consider what steps you can take to acquire them. Continuous learning is important because not only does it help you keep current in your field, but it also improves your self-confidence and career prospects.

Here are some ways you can acquire new skills, improve your existing skills, or gain relevant experience. Use one or more ways to address the unchecked items from your self-assessment above.

- Read books, magazines, and journals.

- Take in-person or online classes.

- Attend conferences, workshops, and mentoring programs.

- Read blogs and sign up for newsletters and RSS feeds.

- Watch videos, podcasts, and webinars.

- Search the Internet.

- Participate in forum discussions.

- Email, call and follow the experts in your field.

- Job shadowing/sharing.

- Volunteer to acquire skills and gain relevant experience.

From here to the end of this chapter, you will learn how to build your CAST profile to give you the best chance of getting the job you want.

Sometimes you may have to use the tasks or responsibilities of your current or previous job to explain your qualifications. In general, however, it is better to use competencies, not job duties, to explain your qualifications. For example, use *"Applied knowledge of case management system to develop a technical guide for staff."* instead of *"Created a technical guide for staff."*

Later you will learn more about this flexible approach and how to use it to present your qualifications and experiences in different ways to apply for different jobs you are qualified to do. This approach is especially helpful when you want to move to another field.

Everything you do requires at least one skill. For example, you need business writing skills to produce reports. You need presentation and persuasion skills to give briefings. To develop a business plan, you need strategic thinking, financial planning, setting performance targets, and many other skills. These skills are your competencies. When you assess the skills you use to perform your daily job tasks, you will discover you have more competencies than you realize. You can learn to transfer them to other types of work.

If you already know how to use your competencies to describe your qualifications and experiences, continue to section 1.4.2.3. Otherwise, use the worksheets in this section and the next any time you need to figure out the competencies behind each task. You will use these worksheets to build your competency map in section 1.4.2.4.

1. List each task that you did in column A.

2. For each task ask the question: **What knowledge, experience, or skills <u>must</u> someone have in order to do this task?** In sections B and C, check off the

applicable competencies (refer to section 1.4.1.4 if needed).

3. List the tangible and intangible products or deliverables (documents, reports, software, a server upgrade...) and tools involved in sections D and E.

For illustration purposes, I am going to use the following three common office tasks to find the competencies required to perform them:

1. Created a technical guide for staff.

2. Presented a business case to managers, executives, and sponsors.

3. Responsible for handling customers' complaints.

(A) Task	(B) Job-specific Competencies												(C) Standard Competencies								
	C1-Technical capability knowledge	C2-Equipment and program knowledge	C3-Customers relationship management	C4-Research	C5-Data analysis	C6-Identifying patterns or connections	C7-Policies	C8-Planning	C9-Business acumen	C10-Speaking and listening	C11-Writing	C12-Computer literacy	C13-Time management	C14-Analytical thinking	C15-Resourcefulness	C16-Communication	C17-Negotiation	C18-Persuasion	C19-Problem solving	C20-Decision making	C21-Commitment
Created a technical guide for staff.	x	x		x								x	x		x	x					x
Presented a business case to managers, executives, and sponsors.		x							x	x						x		x			
Responsible for handling customers' complaints.		x	x						x							x	x		x		x

(D) PRODUCTS/DELIVERABLES

- Technical guide
- Business case

(E) TOOLS

- Microsoft Word
- Microsoft Outlook
- Adobe InDesign

1.4.2.2 Step 2: Can I fit in?

For each task ask the question: **What abilities must someone have in order to do this task?** In section C, check off the applicable competencies (refer to section 1.4.1.4 if needed).

(A) Task	(C) Standard Competencies			
	C22-Interpersonal awareness	C23-Collaboration	C24-Handling pressures and stress	C25-Change management
Created a technical guide for staff.			x	
Presented a business case to managers, executives, and sponsors.	x			
Responsible for handling customers' complaints.	x			

1.4.2.3 Step 3: Can I be trusted?

From the following three competencies, check all the words that describe who you are and what you value. Then, write one or more statements (see examples provided) in the **Statement** column for each selected item that starts with "I" and includes the word or alternate word or form (adjective or noun). You will use these statements in your cover letters as described in section 3.4.

C26-Responsibility and ethics

Word	Statement
☐ Attentive	I believe being *attentive* has helped my continual success in _____.
☐ Capable	
☐ Competent	
☐ Conscientious	
☐ Dedicated	
☐ Dependable	
☐ Diligent	
☐ Discreet	
☐ Dutiful	
☐ Fair	
☐ Honest	

Word	Statement
☐ Impartial	
☐ Meticulous	
☐ Loyal	
☐ Precise	
☐ Punctual	
☐ Respectable	
☐ Tactful	
☐ Trustworthy	

C27-Compliance

Word	Statement
☐ Adaptable	
☐ Coachable	
☐ Friendly	I trust that my *friendliness* fits well with _____.
☐ Helpful	

Word	Statement
☐ Observant	
☐ Perceptive	
☐ Sensitive	
☐ Sociable	
☐ Versatile	

C28-Personal development

Word	Statement
☐ Adventurous	
☐ Ambitious	
☐ Assertive	
☐ Competitive	
☐ Confident	
☐ Courteous	
☐ Decisive	

Word	Statement
☐ Determined	
☐ Eager	I am always *eager* to learn more about _____.
☐ Easygoing	
☐ Energetic	
☐ Enthusiastic	
☐ Empathetic	
☐ Imaginative	
☐ Immaculate	
☐ Independent	
☐ Intelligent	
☐ Intuitive	
☐ Kind	
☐ Loving	
☐ Motivated	

Word	Statement
☐ Optimistic	
☐ Passionate	
☐ Patient	
☐ Perseverant	
☐ Philosophical	
☐ Positive	
☐ Pro-active	
☐ Resilient	
☐ Results-oriented	
☐ Self-disciplined	
☐ Sensible	
☐ Sincere	
☐ Spirited	

1.4.2.4 Step 4: Creating a competency map

A competency map is useful not only to identify the competencies you've gained throughout your career but also to visualize what you need or want to learn and improve.

Refer to section 1.4.1.4, check off and use an adjective to describe each competency you have, including those you've uncovered in sections 1.4.2.1 and 1.4.2.2. Then, create statements by combining adjectives, competency, and, when possible, include keywords from section 3.2 or from the job advertisement. See the following table for sample statements. You will be using these statements in your résumés and cover letters. Use positive adjectives such as these where appropriate:

- Acute
- Advanced
- Competent
- Excellent
- Exceptional
- Exemplary
- Experienced

- Expert
- Extensive
- Outstanding
- Proficient
- Proven
- Qualified
- Remarkable

- Solid
- Strong
- Superb

- Superior
- Talented
- Thorough

	Competency	Adjective	Statement
x	C1-Technical capability	Expert	• Expert *(adjective)* knowledge and skills *(competency)* in IT project management *(keywords)*. • Proficient *(adjective)* in JavaScript, jQuery, PHP, CSS, XHTML, HTML, and XML *(competency)* web technologies *(keywords)*.
x	C2-Equipment and program knowledge		
x	C3-Customer relationship management		
x	C4-Research		
	C5-Data analysis		
	C6-Identifying patterns or connections		
	C7-Policies		
	C8-Planning		
x	C9-Business acumen		
x	C10-Speaking and listening		
x	C11-Writing		
x	C12-Computer literacy		
	C13-Time management		
x	C14-Analytical thinking		
	C15-Resourcefulness		
x	C16-Communication		
x	C17-Negotiation		
x	C18-Persuasion		

	Competency	Adjective	Statement
x	C19-Problem solving		
	C20-Decision making		
x	C21-Commitment		
x	C22-Interpersonal awareness		
x	C23-Collaboration		
	C24-Handling pressures and stress		
	C25-Change management		

As you can see, the exercises up to this point have uncovered 16 competencies behind the three tasks:

1. Created a technical guide for staff.

2. Presented a business case to managers, executives, and sponsors.

3. Responsible for handling customers' complaints.

Some of the competencies you've uncovered are transferable which allows you to present them in different ways. In the next section, you will learn how to write competency-based qualification statements that are results-oriented and attention-grabbing. In a competency-based statement, the competency and results are highlighted instead of the task or product. Such a statement also broadens the scope of the task or product. For example, if you have the knowledge and skills in a certain field and you've only created one technical guide, you could create other documents and presentations too, right?

Here are some samples of task-based and competency-based qualification statements.

Competency	Task-based	Competency-based
C1 Technical capability	Created a technical guide for staff.	**Applied knowledge of case management system** *(competency)* to develop a technical guide for staff that **reduced support calls by 20%** *(result)*.
C2 Equipment and program knowledge	Presented a business case to managers, executives, and sponsors.	**Obtained $1M funding approval** *(result)* by presenting a business case with **analyses and replacement options for the current case management systems** *(competency)* to managers, executives, and sponsors.
C3 Customer relationship management	Responsible for handling customers' complaints.	**Provided customers with suitable solutions** *(competency)* that addressed their complaints **to ensure 100% satisfactory rate** *(result)*.
C16 Communication	Created a technical guide for staff.	**Introduced the new case management system** *(competency)* to staff through a technical guide **which resulted in a 20% reduction in support calls** *(result)*.
C18 Persuasion	Presented a business case to managers, executives, and sponsors.	**Overcame objections** *(competency)* **and secured approval for $1M funding** *(result)* for a business case presented to managers, executives, and sponsors.
C19 Problem solving	Responsible for handling customers' complaints.	**Resolved complaints** *(competency)* from customers in a timely manner to ensure **100% satisfactory rate** *(result)*.

As you can see from the above examples, you can highlight any competency or use it to match the job advertisement requirement. For example, if you wish to highlight your technical knowledge, you'd use C1: *"Applied knowledge of case management system to develop a technical guide for staff that reduced support calls by 20%."* If the job advertisement mentions communication skills, you'd use C16: *"Introduced the new case management system to staff through a technical guide which resulted in a 20% reduction in support calls."*

1.4.2.5 Step 5: Creating qualification statements

You will need to spend the bulk of your time gathering and compiling information about your attitude, education, skills, and experience. This inventory will make your future job hunting process much easier, quicker, and more effective.

Do the following steps for each competency you have in section 1.4.2.4. In later chapters, you will learn how to use this information every time you look for a new job.

For each competency, use the suggestions provided to write your own qualification statements in the **Qualifications** section. Provide a unique number for each statement so you can reference it more easily. Follow the steps below to complete each statement. Switch the order of steps 1 and 2 if necessary.

1. Find past-tense active verbs that summarize what you've accomplished. Use brief phrases. You can find possible verbs in section 6.1 or in a thesaurus. For example, ***Applied knowledge of case management system to develop a technical guide for staff.***

2. When possible, add statistics, percentages, and numbers to the statement to show the impact you've made, results you've delivered, or the magnitude of the responsibility. For example, *Applied knowledge of case management system to develop a technical guide for staff **that reduced support calls by 20%.*** Other examples might include:

   - Managed and achieved project goals with a budget of $_____.

   - Streamlined _____ procedures, shortening process from _____ to _____.

   - An improvement on process, reputation, customer service such as: Improved support service level by _____%.

- A reduction in time, costs, errors such as: Reduced costs from $_____ to $_____ by _____.

- An increase in revenue, customer satisfaction, productivity, collaboration such as: Increased sales by $_____ (or _____ %). (Use the larger number when possible. For example, use $50,000 instead of 10%).

- An elimination of problem, complaint, and waste such as: Eliminated the _____ process.

- A new gain: skill, award, recognition...

3. In the **Where/When** column, put the name of the organization, city and state of its location, and month and year of your employment/involvement where you used that competency. For example, *ABC Company, Toronto, ON, January 2010 - present.* This information is helpful for identifying and sorting information on your résumé.

C1-Technical capability

This competency is about your ability to demonstrate depth of knowledge and skills in a technical area.

SUGGESTIONS

- *Achieved _____, _____, and _____*

- *Administered _____ process including _____, _____, and _____*

- *Applied _____ knowledge to _____ for _____*

- *Attained degree/certification in _____ in/since _____*

- *Compiled and provided _____ to _____*

- *Created _____ for _____ use*

- *Developed _____ solutions to _____*

- *Exhibited thorough knowledge of _____, _____, and _____*

- *Led the _____, _____, and _____ of _____*

- *Performed various _____ duties such as _____*

- *Possessed an in-depth knowledge and skill in _____*

- *Prepared _____ programs for _____*

- *Provided _____ to _____ as a subject matter expert in _____*

- *Retained informed about cutting-edge technology in _____*

- *Reviewed and signed off on _____, _____, and _____*

- *Spent _____ years in _____*

- *Trained _____ on _____*

QUALIFICATIONS	Where/When
Q1.1	
Q1.2	
Q1.3	

C2-Equipment and program knowledge

This competency is about your ability to diagnose equipment or process issues.

SUGGESTIONS

- *Analyzed _____ to provide specification for _____*

- *Applied knowledge in _____ to diagnose _____ issues*

- *Assessed _____ and _____*

- *Designed/developed _____ using _____*

- *Directed and documented the process of _____*

- *Initiated _____ modifications, _____ expansions and _____ releases*

- *Led _____ procedures*

- *Modified _____ by _____*

- *Obtained _____ from _____ by using existing knowledge in _____ to _____*

QUALIFICATIONS	Where/When
Q2.1	
Q2.2	
Q2.3	

C3-Customer relationship management

This competency is about your ability to adopt processes to provide positive interactions with customers, resolve issues, and handle complaints effectively in a timely manner.

SUGGESTIONS

- *Advised customers regarding _____*

- *Assisted customers to _____*

- *Communicated with customers to receive _____*

- *Created and maintained _____ program*

- *Documented reports related to customer's feedback and presented them to (whom) to (do what) in _____*

- *Encouraged referrals by _____*

- *Ensured all customers get positive and delightful experience by _____*

- *Established relationships with new customers by _____*

SUGGESTIONS

- *Evaluated customers' _____ and _____*

- *Facilitated customer feedback through _____ to improve _____*

- *Maintained contact with existing customers through _____, _____, and*

  _____

- *Provided customers with _____, _____, and _____ experience*

- *Provided customers with _____ that _____ to _____*

- *Provided customers with _____ solutions*

- *Provided suggestions for customer improvements to _____*

QUALIFICATIONS   **Where/When**
Q3.1

Q3.2

Q3.3

C4-Research

This competency is about your ability to identify the information needed to clarify a situation, seek that information from appropriate sources, and use skillful questioning to draw out the information when others are reluctant to disclose it.

SUGGESTIONS

- *Completed _____ research in _____*

- *Conducted extensive research to ensure _____*

- *Conducted independent research, including _____, _____, and _____*

- *Identified opportunities/risks in _____*

- *Investigated potential _____ opportunities and made recommendations to*

  _____

- *Kept abreast of _____, _____, and _____*

- *Recommended _____, _____, and _____*

- *Provided research analysis on _____ and _____*

- *Published research findings at _____*

- *Received awards/grants for _____*

- *Researched _____ and _____ to develop effective _____ strategies*

- *Researched _____ and _____ to stay updated on _____ and _____*

- *Researched _____ and used information to _____*

- *Researched _____ regarding _____*

- *Studied _____ for _____*

QUALIFICATIONS   **Where/When**

Q4.1

Q4.2

Q4.3

C5-Data analysis

This competency is about your experience in collecting and analyzing different data sets to obtain business insights.

SUGGESTIONS

- *Analyzed _____ and provided _____*

- *Analyzed _____ to _____*

- *Analyzed and modified _____, including _____, _____, _____*

- *Collected and assembled data for _____*

- *Conducted _____ analysis and provided summaries of analysis*

- *Evaluated _____ and _____*

- *Identified, tracked, reported _____ in _____*

- *Maintained _____ during _____, _____, and _____*

- *Measured _____ based on _____ and _____*

- *Verified _____ and _____*

QUALIFICATIONS   **Where/When**

Q5.1

Q5.2

Q5.3

C6-Identifying patterns or connections

This competency is about your ability to identify underlying issues and trends in complex situations, to locate inconsistencies between situations that are not obviously related, and to use inductive reasoning to form ideas about groups of events or situations.

SUGGESTIONS

- *Analyzed _____ from _____*

- *Assessed _____ by _____*

- *Conducted tests and trial runs to _____*

- *Coordinated with _____ in _____*

- *Developed new _____ techniques*

- *Documented _____ and clarified it with _____*

- *Evaluated the _____ impact of _____*

- *Forecasted _____, _____, and _____*

SUGGESTIONS

- *Implemented _____ and _____ to _____*

- *Measured _____*

- *Monitored _____ and _____ to _____*

- *Produced _____ on _____*

QUALIFICATIONS   Where/When

Q6.1

Q6.2

Q6.3

C7-Policies

This competency is about your knowledge of why policies are important and how they link to business values and cultures.

SUGGESTIONS

- *Designed, interpreted, and conducted a variety of _____ studies to support*

  _____

- *Evaluated existing policy on _____ and recommended _____*

- *Formulated policy on _____*

- *Guided _____ in applying and collecting _____ for _____*

SUGGESTIONS

- *Helped _____ in applying for _____ by including _____ in policy*

- *Implemented necessary changes in _____ after consultation with _____*

- *Represented _____ on _____*

QUALIFICATIONS   Where/When
Q7.1

Q7.2

Q7.3

C8-Planning

This competency is about your ability to identify trends and developments in advance, anticipate stumbling blocks, and developing contingency plans.

SUGGESTIONS

- *Allocated resources to _____ as per _____ and _____*

- *Planned, coordinated, and executed _____*

- *Oversaw the planning and execution of _____ for _____*

- *Supervised production of _____*

QUALIFICATIONS   **Where/When**

Q8.1

Q8.2

Q8.3

C9-Business acumen

This competency is about your ability to analyze the organization's competitive position by considering market and industry trends, existing and potential customers, and strengths and weaknesses compared to competitors. It also includes the ability to look for and seize profitable business opportunities and the willingness to take calculated risks to achieve business goals.

SUGGESTIONS

- *Adopted best industrial practices in _____ to _____*

- *Analyzed and interpreted trends to _____*

- *Forecasted _____ to _____*

- *Learned about the latest _____ from _____*

- *Maintained awareness of _____ trends in the _____ industry*

- *Promoted brand awareness through _____ and _____*

- *Promoted company at _____ and _____*

SUGGESTIONS

- *Represented company at _____ as _____*

- *Supported _____ by researching current and future demands for _____*

QUALIFICATIONS   Where/When
Q9.1

Q9.2

Q9.3

C10-Speaking and listening

This competency is about your ability to speak clearly and listen attentively.

SUGGESTIONS

- *Articulated _____ to _____*

- *Confirmed understanding by _____*

- *Delivered _____ for _____*

- *Elicited _____ on _____*

- *Presented _____ information to _____*

- *Presented _____ for _____ to _____*

- *Used plain talk to explain complex or technical concepts of _____*

SUGGESTIONS

QUALIFICATIONS   **Where/When**

Q10.1

Q10.2

Q10.3

C11-Writing

This competency is about your ability to structure ideas clearly and use concise, clear, appropriate language to convey your ideas succinctly and effectively.

SUGGESTIONS

- *Composed and presented _____ to _____*

- *Composed scripts for _____*

- *Developed copy for _____, _____, and _____*

- *Developed presentations for _____*

- *Helped _____ create effective written material*

- *Posted online well-researched topics on _____ and _____*

- *Prepared _____ statements and _____ responses*

- *Proofread and edited _____*

- *Provided _____, _____, and _____ for _____, _____, and _____*

SUGGESTIONS

- *Translated _____ and _____ into specific copywriting tasks*

QUALIFICATIONS   Where/When
Q11.1

Q11.2

Q11.3

C12-Computer literacy

This competency is about your experience with relevant software packages and the ability to learn new systems quickly.

SUGGESTIONS

- *Certified in _____, _____, and _____*

- *Installed and maintained _____, _____, and _____*

- *Maintained database of _____ records*

- *Operated _____, _____, _____*

- *Provided technical assistance to _____ on a _____ basis*

- *Trained in _____, _____, _____*

- *Updated computer systems with _____ and _____ on a _____ basis*

- *Verified _____ compatibility with _____*

QUALIFICATIONS	Where/When
Q12.1	
Q12.2	
Q12.3	

C13-Time management

This competency is about your ability to use resources effectively to achieve objectives or to prioritize workload to meet deadlines. It is the process of organizing and planning how to divide time between activities to increase efficiency and reduce stress.

SUGGESTIONS

- *Assessed and prioritized _____, _____, and _____*

- *Built _____ and _____ to reflect desired _____ targets*

- *Collected and coordinated _____*

- *Delegated _____ to _____*

- *Developed task checklists to maximize _____ and _____*

- *Estimated _____ timelines and managed _____*

- *Maintained schedules and assured on-time delivery of _____*

- *Managed multiple simultaneous _____ with _____*

SUGGESTIONS

- *Maximized _____ and _____ by _____ and _____*

- *Organized and prioritized _____*

- *Organized _____ and _____ to maximize productivity*

QUALIFICATIONS   **Where/When**

Q13.1

Q13.2

Q13.3

C14-Analytical thinking

This competency is about your ability to break complex tasks into manageable segments and identify potential problems using a logical, systematic, sequential approach to find effective solutions. It is about taking a holistic, abstract, or theoretical perspective; anticipating the implications and consequences of situations; and taking appropriate action to be prepared for possible contingencies.

SUGGESTIONS

- *Analyzed _____ to _____*

- *Analyzed _____ to _____ for _____*

SUGGESTIONS

- *Assessed _____ in order to develop _____ to _____*

- *Assessed current trends in _____ and developed recommendations for*

  _____

- *Assessed problems of _____ by _____, _____, and _____*

- *Completed _____ analysis by assessing _____*

- *Examined _____, _____, and _____ to _____ and _____*

QUALIFICATIONS   Where/When
Q14.1

Q14.2

Q14.3

C15-Resourcefulness

This competency is about your ability to use existing resources or knowledge to devise new ways of working and to tackle unexpected challenges. It is about being open-minded about possibilities and using talents and resources to fulfill goals so that more can be done for less. It is not just for creating something new, but also for improving existing things.

SUGGESTIONS

- *Boosted _____ efficiency by _____*

- *Brainstormed _____ to _____*

- *Composed/wrote _____ to/for _____*

- *Constructed/restructured _____ to _____*

- *Created _____ to/for _____*

- *Designed/redesigned/devised _____ for _____ to _____*

- *Identified _____ and made recommendations for _____*

- *Improved _____ through _____, _____, and _____*

- *Increased _____ by _____*

- *Initiated _____ to _____ and _____*

- *Intervened in _____ to prevent _____ or improve _____*

- *Managed _____ by _____ and _____*

- *Monitored _____ and optimized _____ to _____*

- *Proposed/suggested _____ to/for _____*

- *Recommended _____ to increase _____ and reduce _____*

- *Reduced and controlled _____ by _____*

QUALIFICATIONS	Where/When
Q15.1	
Q15.2	
Q15.3	

C16-Communication

This competency is about your ability to use appropriate tools and languages to explain information clearly and concisely and to express emotions appropriately.

SUGGESTIONS

- *Communicated _____ to _____*

- *Consulted with _____ to _____*

- *Described _____ and demonstrated _____ of _____*

- *Discussed _____ with _____ to assess _____*

- *Drafted _____ highlighting _____, _____, and _____*

- *Introduced _____ to _____*

- *Managed communications and presentations with regards to _____, _____, and _____*

- *Presented _____ to _____*

SUGGESTIONS

- *Promoted _____ by communicating with _____, _____, and _____*

- *Provided information concerning _____, _____, and _____*

- *Used _____, _____, and _____ to _____*

QUALIFICATIONS   Where/When
Q16.1

Q16.2

Q16.3

C17-Negotiation

This competency is about your ability to address key concerns and present mutually beneficial solutions intended to reach an understanding or agreement.

SUGGESTIONS

- *Discussed options with _____ to _____*

- *Initiated negotiations regarding _____*

- *Negotiated _____, _____, and _____*

- *Negotiated _____ as per the _____, _____, and _____ constraints*

- *Negotiated details of _____ with _____ and _____*

SUGGESTIONS

- *Negotiated with _____ to _____*

- *Obtained the best _____ and _____*

QUALIFICATIONS   Where/When
Q17.1

Q17.2

Q17.3

C18-Persuasion

This competency is about your ability to use audience-specific language and examples to present arguments to illustrate and support your own positions in order to gain others' support.

SUGGESTIONS

- *Acquired _____ in _____ (time)*

- *Developed new _____ scripts/techniques to _____*

- *Overcame objections and secured _____*

QUALIFICATIONS   **Where/When**
Q18.1

Q18.2

Q18.3

C19-Problem solving

This competency is about your ability to identify and analyze the causes and effects of problems and to develop appropriate solutions using logic, judgment, and data.

SUGGESTIONS

- *Dealt with _____ issues such as _____, _____, and _____*

- *Resolved _____, _____, and _____ issues*

- *Resolved _____ from _____ in a timely manner*

- *Solved _____ issues related to _____ and _____*

- *Responded to and resolved _____ as required*

QUALIFICATIONS   **Where/When**
Q19.1

Q19.2

Q19.3

C20-Decision making

This competency is about your ability to prioritize different needs and analyze data and information to make considered decisions in a timely manner.

SUGGESTIONS

- *Assessed the impact of the decision on _____ and modified _____ to _____*

- *Defined _____, generated _____, and evaluated_____*

- *Provided timely decisions for _____*

- *Selected _____ and implemented _____*

- *Solicited information from _____, _____, and _____ to make informed decisions regarding _____*

QUALIFICATIONS	Where/When
Q20.1	
Q20.2	
Q20.3	

C21-Commitment

This competency is about your ability to produce high-quality work that meets or exceeds the organization's requirements and seek new ways to improve productivity.

SUGGESTIONS

- *Administered audits to verify _____ and _____*

- *Ascertained _____ and _____*

- *Conducted quality checks on _____*

- *Conducted quality reviews of _____ to ensure compliance with _____*

- *Demonstrated a continued commitment to _____ through _____*

- *Developed standards of best practice for _____*

- *Enabled proper utilization of _____*

- *Ensured all _____ duties were completed including _____ and _____*

- *Ensured that _____, _____, _____ are met*

- *Ensured that _____ and _____ were _____*

- *Followed proper procedures for _____*

- *Maintained accurate records of _____*

- *Maintained high levels of _____, _____, and _____ to ensure quality*

- *Managed production of quality reviews including _____, _____, and*

SUGGESTIONS

_____

- *Monitored _____ and take appropriate action to ensure _____ quality and _____ standards are consistently met*

- *Performed _____ to ensure that _____*

- *Performed _____ to gauge _____ and _____*

QUALIFICATIONS   Where/When
Q21.1

Q21.2

Q21.3

C22-Interpersonal awareness

This competency is about your ability to recognize and regulate your own emotions and behaviours and to recognize and respect others' emotions and perspectives.

SUGGESTIONS

- *Collaborated and cooperated with _____ on _____*

- *Adapted _____ to _____*

- *Promoted _____ awareness to _____*

SUGGESTIONS

- *Embraced diversity, empathy, and understanding in _____*

QUALIFICATIONS   Where/When

Q22.1

Q22.2

Q22.3

C23-Collaboration

This competency is about your ability to build strong relationships through honest communication, active sharing, participation, and cooperation.

SUGGESTIONS

- *Assisted _____ in _____ to _____*

- *Assisted _____ by _____*

- *Collaborated with _____ and maintained positive relationship to _____ and _____*

- *Conducted _____ with _____ on _____*

- *Coordinated with _____ to _____*

SUGGESTIONS

- *Held meetings and discussions with _____ to _____*

- *Interacted with _____, _____, and _____*

- *Maintained constant contact with _____ to _____ and _____*

- *Networked in _____ to _____*

- *Partnered with _____ to _____*

- *Participated in _____ and _____ with _____ to _____*

- *Reviewed _____ and suggested required changes*

- *Supervised _____ to ensure _____*

- *Traded _____ with _____ to ensure _____ success*

- *Worked with _____ to _____ that might influence _____*

QUALIFICATIONS   Where/When
Q23.1

Q23.2

Q23.3

C24-Handling pressures and stress

This competency is about your ability to manage feelings or symptoms of stress and respond calmly to criticism.

SUGGESTIONS

- *Handled multiple _____ concurrently*

- *Incorporated feedback into _____*

- *Skilled at balancing multiple _____ and _____*

- *Thrived under _____ and consistently _____*

QUALIFICATIONS   Where/When
Q24.1

Q24.2

Q24.3

C25-Change management

This competency is about your ability to embrace, support, and promote organizational change or to help others manage the emotional impact of change.

SUGGESTIONS

- *Assessed _____ and _____ continuously and made changes as needed to _____*

- *Implemented _____ to _____*

- *Initiated changes to improve _____*

SUGGESTIONS

- *Managed the process of designing and implementing new _____*

- *Monitored and tracked _____ to determine effectiveness and determine future changes*

QUALIFICATIONS	Where/When
Q25.1	
Q25.2	
Q25.3	

C26-Responsibility and ethics

This competency is about your ability to take responsibility for your own actions and mistakes, respect values and confidential agreements, and demonstrate high standards of ethical conduct and behaviours consistent with the organization's policies.

SUGGESTIONS

- *Adhered to _____*

- *Fulfilled _____, _____, and _____*

- *Maintained confidentiality of _____ and any sensitive situations*

- *Observed _____ and _____*

SUGGESTIONS

- *Supported _____ to _____*

QUALIFICATIONS   **Where/When**
Q26.1

Q26.2

Q26.3

C27-Compliance

This competency is about your ability to recognize and support the organization's structure, policies, and its value of diversity.

SUGGESTIONS

- *Developed procedures for _____*

- *Exhibited expert knowledge of policies, procedures, and ethical standards regarding _____*

- *Implemented _____ to support _____*

- *Monitored _____ and _____ for conformance with _____ goals*

- *Oversaw _____ to ensure compliance with _____ procedures and _____ guidelines*

SUGGESTIONS

- *Performed _____ that are in compliance with corporate policies, practices, and procedures*

- *Promoted and advocated _____ and _____ across the _____*

- *Trained and mentored _____ in _____ protocols, _____ issues, and _____ compliance*

- *Supervised _____ for following protocols regarding _____ and _____*

QUALIFICATIONS   **Where/When**
Q27.1

Q27.2

Q27.3

C28-Personal development

This competency is about your ability to take responsibility for your own performance, by setting clear goals and expectations, tracking progress against the goals, ensuring feedback, and addressing performance problems and issues promptly. It is also about personality and those drivers that influence thinking, feeling and behaviour.

SUGGESTIONS

- *Attended _____ to maintained knowledge on _____*

- *Established _____ and exceeded in _____*

- *Excelled at _____*

- *Learned and stayed abreast of _____*

QUALIFICATIONS   **Where/When**

Q28.1

Q28.2

Q28.3

1.4.2.6 Step 6: Creating CAR stories

During interviews, hiring managers will ask questions to assess your claims of the skills and expertise you bring to a role. Some questions may require examples from your previous experience. These are often about the standard competencies (C13 to C28). Answering these questions in a story format can deliver a compelling message and demonstrate that you are the best candidate for the job.

In section 4.4 you will learn how to use stories in interviews. In this section, you are going to write stories about your experiences at work (or personal experience if you need to) using the CAR technique. CAR stands for Context (or Circumstance), Action, and Result. This technique, also referred to as PAR (Problem identification, Action explanation, and Results achieve) or STAR (Situation, Task, Action, and Results), uses structured stories to illustrate competencies.

To describe your own experiences using the CAR technique, answer the following questions:

PART	INCLUDE
Context: Describe the situation, task, or problem.	• What was the situation/task/problem?
	• How large, complex, and/or important was the situation/task/problem?
	• What was your role in dealing with the situation/task/problem?
	• Which tasks or responsibilities were

PART	INCLUDE

assigned to you?

- What was your accountability and scope of decision-making?

Action: Describe the actions you took or would take to evade the situation, complete the task, or solve the problem.

- What did you do?
- How did you do it? This is your chance to demonstrate your knowledge of methodologies and your skills. For example, "I used this *(methodology)* and went through these *(phases/stages/steps)*. I ran into these *(challenges/issues)* and overcame them using these *(competencies and techniques)*." If you want to demonstrate your analytical skills and/or good judgement, you can also provide a reason for your action. Help the interviewer to see the connection between your skills and your action. For example, "I had to use my _____ skills to _____."

PART	INCLUDE

or "Communication, facilitation, and persuasion skills were necessary to achieving consensus. I called a meeting and used techniques _____, _____, and _____ to get everyone on board."

Result: Describe the result of your actions, focusing on how your actions resulted in a success for the organization.

- What was the result? For example, "The project came in on time and on budget and I won a project management award." or something you've learned or would have done differently. The result can also be:

  - An improvement on process, reputation, customer service.

  - A reduction in time, costs, errors.

  - An increase in revenue, customer satisfaction, productivity, collaboration.

  - An elimination of problem,

PART   **INCLUDE**

complaint, waste.

- A new gain: skill, award, recognition.

- How would this experience contribute to the job you are applying? (This is optional but you would make an excellent impression if you could include it).

Use the structure above with the sample template below to write your stories. Briefly state the CONTEXT then focus 60-70% on the ACTIONS and the remainder on the RESULT. Select from the following common scenarios or add your own. Write at least one story for each relevant competency. You may use the same story for multiple competencies when it is fitting. Provide a unique number for each story so you can refer to it later in the process.

Over time, you can add or change your stories. The more stories you have, the better they prepare you for interviews. After you set up your CAST profile with these stories, update it annually or when needed.

Sample template

S13.1   A story about a time I had to be strategic in order to meet all my top priorities.

C

A

R

C13-Time management

S13.1   A story about a time I had to be strategic in order to meet all my top priorities.

S13.2   A story about a time I had to keep everything moving along in a timely manner for a long-term project.

S13.3   A story about a time my responsibilities got a little overwhelming.

C14-Analytical thinking

S14.1   A story about a time I had to analyze information and make a recommendation.

C15-Resourcefulness

S15.1   A story about a time I came up with a new approach to a problem.

S15.2   A story about a time I found a creative way to overcome an obstacle.

S15.3   A story about a time I had to think on my feet in order to delicately extricate myself from a difficult or awkward situation.

C16-Communication

S16.1   A story about a time I gave a successful presentation.

S16.2   A story about a time I had to explain something fairly complex to a frustrated client.

S16.3   A story about a time I had to relay bad news to a client or colleague.

S16.4   A story about a time I had to rely on written communication to get my ideas across.

C17-Negotiation

S17.1   A story about a time I had to consider different peoples' perspectives when exploring an issue.

S17.2   A story about a time I had to arrive at a compromise or help others to compromise.

S17.3   A story about a time I had to consider the sensitivities of different parties.

C18-Persuasion

S18.1 A story about a time I faced opposition when I tried to introduce something.

S18.2 A story about a time I made a point that I knew my colleagues would be resistant to.

S18.3 A story about a time I was able to successfully persuade someone to see things my way at work.

C19-Problem solving

S19.1 A story about a time I anticipated potential problems and developed preventive measures.

S19.2 A story about a time I had to solve a problem but didn't have all the necessary information about it in hand.

S19.3 A story about a time I handled a difficult situation or assignment.

C20-Decision making

S20.1 A story about the toughest decision I ever had to make.

S20.2 A story about a time I had to make a decision without all the information I needed.

S20.3   A story about a time I had to reach a decision quickly.

C21-Commitment

S21.1   A story about a time I saw a problem and took initiative to correct it.

S21.2   A story about a time I went above and beyond the call of duty at work.

C22-Interpersonal awareness

S22.1   A story about a time I had to work with someone unhappy.

S22.2   A story about a time I was dissatisfied in my work.

C23-Collaboration

S23.1   A story about a time I disagreed with my supervisor/manager.

S23.2   A story about a time I faced a difficult situation with a co-worker.

S23.3   A story about a time I had a conflict with my supervisor/manager.

S23.4   A story about a time I had to give someone difficult feedback.

S23.5 A story about a time I had to work closely with someone whose personality was very different from mine.

S23.6 A story about a time I handled a team member who was not pulling his/her own weight.

S23.7 A story about a time I needed to get information from someone who wasn't very responsive.

S23.8 A story about a time I responded to a colleague putting me down at work.

S23.9 A story about a time I struggled to build a relationship with someone important.

S23.10 A story about a time I worked on a team that did not get along.

S23.11 A story about a time I worked on a team with individuals from different cultural backgrounds.

C24-Handling pressure and stress

S24.1 A story about a time I had to cope with strict deadlines or time demands.

S24.2 A story about a time I managed the constant changes that my job demanded.

C25-Change management

S25.1   A story about a time I have to learn something new.

S25.2   A story about a time my manager asked me to implement a different way of working but didn't explain why.

S25.3   A story about a time I had to adjust to changes over which I had no control.

S25.4   A story about a time I had to adjust to a colleague's working style in order to complete a project or achieve my objectives.

C26-Responsibility and ethics

S26.1   A story about a time my integrity was challenged.

S26.2   A story about a time I disagreed with a rule or approach.

C27-Compliance

S27.1   A story about a time I conformed to a policy with which I did not agree.

C28-Personal development

S28.1   A story about a time I addressed criticism of my work.

S28.2 A story about a time I misunderstood an important communication on the job.

S28.3 A story about a time I set a goal for myself and ensuring that I would meet my objective.

1.4.3 Personal brand

Personal branding is about projecting the kind of impression you want and the value you have. A well-crafted personal brand can help you promote yourself through conversations, résumés, business cards, and websites (your own and social networking sites).

A branding statement is a statement connecting your experience to your values and your goal. Follow the instructions below to create your personal branding statement.

1.4.3.1 How to create your personal brand statement

1. Pick one or two professional values that matter most to you. For example, *innovation and experimentation.*

2. Pick one professional goal you want to achieve. For example, *lead teams in the health sector.*

3. Pick a past experience that links your professional values and your professional goal. For example, *over 20 years in delivering innovative, complex, and large-scale IT solutions.*

Sample of a personal brand statement:

> *A senior project manager with over 20 years of experience in delivering innovative, complex, and large-scale IT solutions pursuing a career in leading revolutionizing teams working on cutting-edge designs and technologies in the health sector.*

Now that you have your CAST profile created, it's time to look in places where you can find your next job.

2. FINDING THE BETTER JOB

In this chapter, we will explore places you can look for jobs, set up your job search strategy, and research companies that you are interested in working with.

2.1   Where to find the better job

2.1.1   Current job

Besides doing your current job exceptionally well so that people will notice your potential, always put yourself in a position to expand your skill set. Look for challenging assignments that build your strength. Take relevant training opportunities and volunteer for projects, including charity campaigns. Project work is an excellent way to build skills and relationships in a short time.

If you want to work on a special project, tell your manager that you're going to talk to the project managers about helping on the side.

You never know where new opportunities will arise when you start taking ownership over your situation. Offer to help and ask for help as needed. If you don't get the answers that you are looking for, start asking other people or start asking different questions.

2.1.2   Current network

Almost anyone you know can recommend jobs or job listing websites. Personal connections can be the best way to find a job because you may get recommended for a job that is not even advertised. A simple conversation can lead to a new contact or even an opportunity for a new job.

Make a list of the people in your network that includes:

- Adult family members
- Friends
- Current and past neighbours
- Current and past co-workers

- Current and past managers

- Current and past classmates

- Current and past associations (e.g. church, gym, social media, community groups)

- Current and past casual acquaintances (e.g. doctor, accountant, landlord, lawyer, hairstylist)

- Current and past connections of family members and friends (e.g. their co-workers, partners, spouses, colleagues, and managers).

Networking is about building genuine relationships, not about using other people or aggressively promoting yourself. It is about helping others as well as helping yourself. Reach out and let the people in your network know what kind of work you're looking for and ask them if they have any information or know anyone in a relevant field.

2.1.3 Job advertisements

Although job websites are more common now, some companies still use local daily newspaper classified advertisements to list job openings. You may also find job flyers posted in public places such as supermarkets, libraries, and community centres.

2.1.4   Job websites

There are many job search websites, but they're not all created equally. Some offer better usability, site features, and specific search requirements while others include outdated job listings and site functionalities. From websites that list local, national, and international jobs to websites that list industry-, sector-, and level-specific jobs, each offers different free and/or paid features such as:

- Search jobs by company, keyword, location, and job title.

- Access to job hunting tips, guides, and articles.

- Access to tools and advice on job interviews or résumé writing.

- Allow users to create an account, save searches and upload résumés, and create email alerts.

- Allow potential employees and employers to make direct contact.

- Featured listings of résumés and applications.

This website https://www.betterteam.com/job-posting-sites provides comprehensive listings of job websites. Many government websites list or link to jobs too. Participation in social network websites such as LinkedIn, Facebook, and Twitter also provide leads to job openings.

2.1.5 Employment agencies and search firms

Employment agencies and search firms provide matching services between employers and employees for a fee. This fee may be paid entirely by the employer or by the employee, or they may split it. The employer may pay the employee directly or through the agency. It may be a lump sum or a rate above what you will be getting. Some agencies specialize in a particular field.

When you go through these agencies, you get access to positions that may not be offered elsewhere, opportunities to explore the possibility of permanent relationships with different employers, and chances to practise your interview skills.

2.1.6 Walk-ins and cold calls

Sometimes it is possible to apply for a job by visiting the office or calling at the right time. As some jobs are not listed or the opening is new, you may get better results. Or, you may get rejected quickly. Consider writing a letter before calling or visiting.

2.1.7 Job fairs

A job fair, also commonly called a career fair or career expo is an in-person or online event in which job seekers can find out information from many companies or organizations in one location. Prospective employees can meet with recruiters to get clarification about qualifications and expectations, leave résumés, or file applications.

2.1.8 Job clubs

A job club, also known as a job search club or a networking club, is a formal or informal group of job seekers helping one another. Job club types and functions vary from informal clubs open to everyone to formal ones for specific groups of people.

Members get opportunities to make connections, share résumés and cover letters, conduct mock interviews, recommend job leads, and offer general encouragement and advice about job search.

Find local job clubs through your local newspaper or websites such as the local chamber of commerce, public libraries, community colleges, local universities, and social networking websites.

You can also start your own job club by either placing an advertisement in your local paper, job search websites or gathering a few friends together for a weekly meeting.

2.2   Job search strategy

Now that you know of the places where you could find a job, use the following checklist to help you come up with your overall job search strategy.

2.2.1   Checklist: Job search strategy

☐ Have I defined what I'm looking for?

☐ Are my goals actionable, achievable, and realistic?

☐ Are my timelines achievable and realistic?

☐ How do I stay focused on what I really want?

☐ Which activities give me the most satisfaction?

☐ What skills am I using that are not reflected on my résumé?

☐ What skills on my résumé am I not using?

☐ What are some skills that I want to acquire or develop?

☐ Which job fields are going to get my targeted efforts?

☐ Do I have a list of organizations I am most interested in working for?

☐ Do I know where to find the people I want to work with?

☐ Do I have a plan to meet with people that could help me?

☐ If applicable, do I have a list of field-related professional organizations, publications, and journals I can research?

☐ Do I have a list of sources where I can research the organizations? For example, websites, annual reports, marketing materials, media articles and press releases, social networks.

☐ Do I have a log of research and activities so I know when and whom I've contacted and the next steps?

2.3   Company research

Researching a company is part of the job-search process and it is usually done before creating your résumés and cover letters. Prior research helps you pitch your application and perform better at the interview. Use the following checklist for each organization where you apply for a job.

2.3.1   Checklist: Company research

☐ Do I know what the organization does?

☐ Do I know about the organization's products/services?

☐ Do I know the company's history?

☐ Do I know the principals/founders who work there?

☐ Do I know what the organization's challenges are?

☐ Do I know who the organization's competitors are?

☐ Do I know the organization's place in the market?

☐ Do I know what the organization cares about?

☐ Do I know if the organization donates to what causes or charities?

☐ Do I know which of their core values resonate with me?

☐ Has the organization been in the news recently?

☐ Are there any rumours about the organization?

☐ Is the organization struggling?

☐ Do I know any inside scoop?

☐ Has the organization been recognized for something?

☐ Do I know how the organization presents itself on social media?

Getting a job is a series of steps. Every step needs to lead you to the job offer. The next step is writing your résumé (or curriculum vitae or CV) and cover letter. Let's get into how to create effective résumés and cover letters, including using your qualification statements from your CAST profile.

3. WRITING A RÉSUMÉ

Résumés are competency-based whereas CVs are credential-based and are often used for jobs in academia, scientific research, and medical fields. Both are personal marketing documents intended to showcase the candidate's skills, achievements, and work experience. CVs provide a comprehensive listing of academic background, certifications, awards, research experience, professional affiliations, and professional memberships.

Before applying for a job, make sure you have the level of education and experience that the job requires. Also, be sure you live in the same geographic area as the job being offered unless the company considers relocating candidates.

Your résumé is basically a sales letter in which you are both the seller and the product. It is a screening tool and its purpose is to get you an interview. An effective résumé should pique the interest of the person who is reading it, show that you are a close match to the criteria he/she is looking for, and make him/her want them to find out more about you. Your résumé should be truthful, but it's up to you to decide what to include or not include and how to present it to best reflect you and your qualifications. Assess every piece of information before including it. Avoid irrelevant details or those tasks that you don't want to end up doing. For example, don't include typing speed if the job does not require it or filing if you don't ever want to do it again.

Your first step is to convince the reader that your résumé is worth reading. It's unlikely that someone is going to read your job history if the résumé looks sloppy and unprofessional, let alone taking its content seriously. Focus on quality and clarity instead of layout and length (unless the job posting requests a specific layout or limits the number of pages).

3.1 Types of résumé

Listed below are three common types of résumé: Chronological, functional, and infographic. Most other formats are variations of these three. Use the résumé type that best emphasizes your skills and qualifications.

3.1.1 Chronological

This is the most common résumé type because it's easy to see your work history. In a chronological (also known as traditional) résumé, your most recent position is listed first and below it are other jobs in reverse chronological order. This type of résumé works well if you have a strong, solid work history. If you often change careers or have gaps in your employment history, list the reasons for short job stints next to the dates (for example, mass layoffs, redundant position, defunct company). Doing so removes the potential doubt that you would stay long in a job.

3.1.2 Functional

A functional (also called a skills-oriented or non-chronological) résumé focuses on your skills and experience instead of work history. It may include a concise work history at the bottom or may not include it at all. This type of résumé works well with the

CAST method and also if you are new to the workforce, often change careers, or have gaps in your employment history.

3.1.3   Infographic

An infographic résumé includes graphic design elements in addition to or instead of text. It uses layout, color, design, formatting, icons, and font styling to organize work experience, education, and skills. Except when you are applying for an artistic job, avoid using this type of résumé unless you are asked to provide one and you have designing skills. It can be hard to pull off a great infographic résumé. It can also be missed in the job application process if the company uses software to scan résumés.

3.2   Keywords

Many companies nowadays use software to manage applications and candidates. Unless you're personally handing your résumé to the hiring manager, it's possible an ATS (Applicant Tracking System) will be used in the applicant screening process. The software sorts, scans, and searches through thousands of résumés, to determine which ones are the best fit. ATS software can score résumés based on a variety of criteria including keywords pre-programmed into the system. Every keyword has a point value. After the ATS system finds the keywords in your résumés, it assigns a score. The hiring team will review the résumés with the highest scores.

In the following sections, I've included keyword lists to use in résumés and cover letters. Make a list of keywords from the job ad and keywords from one of the checklists below that fit your experience for the job you are applying for. For example, if you are applying for a project manager position, pick the most relevant and important keywords from the **Project management** list.

3.2.1 Business Development, Customer Service, Marketing, Sales

Account development • Account management • Account relationship management • Account retention • Brand development • Brand management • Brand positioning • Budgeting • Business development • Call center operations • Campaign management • Change management • Client relationship management • Client research • Closing strategies • Cold calling • Competitive analysis • Competitive market intelligence • Competitive product positioning • Consultative sales • Content development • Customer communications • Customer development • Customer focus groups • Customer loyalty • Customer management • Customer needs assessment • Customer retention • Customer satisfaction • Customer service • Customer surveys • Dashboards • Direct mail marketing • Direct response marketing • Direct sales • Distributor management • E-business • Emerging markets • Expense forecasting • Field sales management • Field service operation • Focus groups • Fulfillment • Global markets • Global sales • Inbound service operation • Indirect sales • Industry research • International sales • International trade • Key account management • Key Performance Indicators (KPIs) • Leadership • Margin improvement • Market launch Market positioning • Market research • Market surveys • Marketing strategy • Metrics progress tracking • Multi-channel distribution • Multi-channel sales • Multimedia advertising • Multimedia marketing communications • National account management • Negotiations • New market development • New product introduction • Order fulfillment • Order processing • Outbound service operation • Process simplification • Product development • Product launch • Product lifecycle management • Product line rationalization • Product positioning • Product pricing • Profit & Loss (P&L) management • Profit growth • Promotions • Public relations • Public speaking • Records management • Relationship management • Revenue growth • Revenue stream • ROI calculations • Sales administration • Sales closing • Sales cycle management • Sales forecasting • Sales presentations • Sales team collaboration • Sales training • Search Engine Optimization (SEO) • Service benchmarks • Service delivery • Social media • Solutions selling • Strategic planning • Team building • Telemarketing operations • Territory management • Trend analysis

3.2.2   Executive Functions

Accelerated growth • Benchmarking • Business development • Business reengineering • Change management • Competitive market position • Consensus building • Continuous process improvement • Corporate communications • Corporate culture change • Corporate development • Corporate legal affairs • Corporate mission/vision • Cost reduction • Crisis communications • Cross-cultural communications • Cross-functional team leadership • Customer-driven management • Decision-making authority • Emerging business venture • Enterprise management • Executive presentations • Financial management • Financial restructuring • Global market expansion • Infrastructure • Leadership development • Margin improvement • Market development • Market-driven management • Marketing management • Matrix management • Multi-site operations management • New business development • Operating infrastructure • Organization/Organizational culture • Organization/Organizational development • Policy development • Performance improvement • Process improvement • Profit & Loss (P&L) management • Profit growth • Project management • Quality improvement • Relationship management • Reengineering • Reorganization • Return on Assets (ROA) • Return on Equity (ROE) • Return on Investment (ROI) • Revenue growth • Sales management • Servant leadership • Start-up venture • Strategic development • Strategic partnership • Team building • Team leadership • Total Quality Management (TQM) • Transition management

3.2.3   Finance

Accounts payable • Accounts receivable • Asset disposition • Asset management • Asset purchase • Audit controls • Audit management • Capital budgets • Cash management • Corporate credit • Corporate tax • Cost accounting • Cost avoidance • Cost reduction • Cost/benefit analysis • Credit & collections • Debt financing • Divestiture • Due diligence • E-commerce • E-trade • Equity financing • Expense tracking • Feasibility analysis • Financial analysis • Financial audits • Financial controls • Financial models • Financial planning • Financial reporting • Foreign Exchange (FX) • Forecasting • Initial Public Offering (IPO) •

Internal controls • International finance • Investment management • Investor accounting • Investor relations • Job costing • Letters of credit • Liability management • Make/buy analysis • Margin improvement • Merger & acquisition • Operating budgets • Profit/Loss (P&L) analysis • Profit gains • Project accounting • Project financing • Regulatory compliance auditing • Return on Assets (ROA) • Return on Equity (ROE) • Return on Investment (ROI) • Revenue gain • Risk management • Stock purchase • Strategic planning • Trust accounting

3.2.4 General business

Benchmarking • Business development • Business reengineering • Change management • Competitive market position • Consensus building • Continuous process improvement • Corporate communications • Corporate culture change • Corporate development • Corporate legal affairs • Corporate mission • Cost avoidance • Cost reduction • Crisis communications • Cross-cultural communications • Cross-functional team leadership • Decision-making authority • E-commerce • Efficiency improvement • Enterprise management • Financial management • Financial restructuring • Global markets • Long-range planning • Margin improvement • Market development • Marketing management • Matrix management • Multi-industry experience • Multi-site operations management • New business development • Operating infrastructure • Operating management • Policy development • Performance improvement • Process reengineering • Productivity improvement • Profit & Loss (P&L) management • Profit growth • Project management • Quality assurance • Quality improvement • Relationship management • Reengineering • Reorganization • Return on Assets (ROA) • Return on Equity (ROE) • Return on Investment (ROI) • Revenue growth • Sales management • Service delivery • Service design • Signatory authority • Start-up venture • Strategic development • Strategic partnership • Tactical leadership • Tactical planning • Team building • Team leadership

3.2.5 Health care administration

Budgeting • Coaching • Compliance • Conducting surveys • Controlling expenses • Cost analysis • Cost per patient • Customer service • Data analysis • Facility management • Financial management • Fundraising • Health care issues • Health insurance processing • Healthcare billing • Healthcare policies and procedures • Healthcare regulations • Hiring • Human resources management • Insurance • Interviewing • Investigating • Key Performance Indicators (KPIs) • Marketing • Medical billing • Medical facility inspections • Medical records processing • Medical services delivery • Medical terminology • Meeting facilitation • Negotiating contracts • Operations management • Patient advocacy • Patient confidentiality • Patient grievances • Performance management • Physician relationships • Presenting • Program management • Project management •

Purchasing • Quality control • Recruiting • Reporting • Research • Scheduling • Social services • Staff evaluation • Strategic planning • Training • Treatment alternatives • Treatment services

3.2.6   Human resources

360 reviews • Assessments • Benefits administration • Change management • College recruitment • Compensation • Competency-based performance • Contract negotiations • Corporate culture • Diversity and inclusion • Employee communications • Employee handbook development • Employee relations • Employee retention • Employee surveys • Executive compensation • Global workforce • Grievance proceedings • Human Resources (HR) • Investigations • Interviewing • Job description development • Labour relations • Leadership assessment • Leadership development • Management training & development • Multimedia training • Onboarding • Organization/Organizational design • Organization/Organizational Development (OD) • Organization/Organizational needs assessment • Performance appraisal • Performance incentives • Performance reengineering • Personnel development plans • Policy development • Position classification • Recognition • Recruitment • Retention • Safety training • Sexual harassment investigations • Staffing • Succession planning • Talent development • Train-the-trainer • Training & development • Union negotiations • Union relations • Virtual workforce management • Wage & salary administration • Workers compensation/Comp administration • Workforce redeployment

3.2.7   Information technology

Active directory • Agile methodologies • Applications development • Architecture • Artificial Intelligence (AI) • Automated Voice Response (AVR) • Benchmarking • Business continuity • Capacity planning • Client/server architecture • Cross-functional technology team • Data communications • Data center operations • Data mining • Data recovery • Database administration • Database design • Database server • Desktop technology • Disaster recovery • Document imaging • E-commerce • E-learning • Electronic Data Interchange (EDI) • Emerging technologies • End user support • Enterprise systems • Ethernet • Extranet • Fault analysis • Fiber optics • Field support • Firewall • Frame relay • Geographic Information System (GIS) • Global systems support • Graphical User Interface (GUI) • Hardware configuration • Hardware development • Hardware engineering • Help desk • Host-based system • Human Resources Information Systems (HRIS) • Imaging technology • Information Systems (IS) • Information Technology (IT) • Internet • Intranet • Internet of Things (IoT) • IT project lifecycle • IT project management • Joint Application Development (JAD) • Legacy systems • Local Area Network (LAN) • Mainframe • Management Information

Systems (MIS) • Mobile technology • Multimedia technology • Multiuser interface • Multivendor systems integration • Network administration • Networking • Object oriented • Office Automation (OA) Offline • Online • Operating system(s) • Parallel systems operations • Pilot implementation • Process modeling • Project lifecycle • Project management methodology • Project scheduling • Rapid Application Development (RAD) • Real time data • Relational database • Remote Systems Access (RAS) • Research & Development (R&D) • Resource management • Satellite communications • Scrum • Six Sigma • Smart technology • Software configuration • Software development • Software engineering • Switches and routers • Systems acquisition • Systems analysis • Systems configuration • Systems development methodology • Systems documentation • Systems engineering • Systems functionality • Systems implementation • Systems integration • Systems migrations • Systems security • Technical documentation • Technical training • Technical writing • Technology commercialization • Technology integration • Technology licensing • Technology needs assessment • Technology rightsizing • Technology solutions • Technology transfer • User training & support • Vendor management • Voice communications • Web hosting • Webcasting • Wide Area Network (WAN)

3.2.8 Non-profit, social services, program management

Annual campaign • Audits • Budgeting • Board relations • Board support • Capital campaign • Case management • Client advocacy • Client resources • Community engagement • Community outreach • Compliance • Data analysis • Database management • Development • Diversity and inclusion • Diverse community outreach • Documentation • Donor communications • Donor management • Expense tracking • External relations • Fundraising • Fundraising events • Government relations • Grant administration • Grant management • Grant writing • Key Performance Indicators (KPIs) • Low income populations • Marketing • Media • Non-profit administration • Partnership development • Policy and procedure development • Policy and procedure implementation • Press releases • Program assessment • Program implementation • Program management • Program performance measurements • Quality assurance • Reporting • Research • Resource allocation • Silent auctions • Social services • Strategic planning • Training • Volunteer management • Volunteer onboarding • Volunteer recruitment • Volunteer training

3.2.9 Office administration

Administrative infrastructure • Administrative processes • Administrative support • Administrative technology • Agenda creation • Back office operations • Board administration • Board support • Budget administration • Calendaring • Client communications • Confidential correspondence • Contract administration •

Corporate recordkeeping • Customer service • Data entry • Document management systems • Efficiency improvement • Event management • Executive liaison • Executive communications • Expense reporting • Facilities management • Filing systems • Front office operations • Government affairs • IT coordination • Liaison affairs • Mail & messenger services • Meeting planning & coordination • Meeting minutes • Multi-line phone operations • Negotiations • Office administration • Office automation • Office management • Office moving • Office relocation • Office supply ordering and tracking • Office technology • Office services • Policies & procedures • Product support • Productivity improvement • Project management • Records management • Regulatory reporting • Resource management • Scheduling • Social media • Training • Travel coordination • Travel planning • Technical support • Time management • Vendor management • Website management • Workflow planning/prioritization

3.2.10 Project management

Agile • Analysis • Budget development • Budget management • Budget planning • Budgeting • Client relations • Collaboration • Communication • Compliance • Conflict resolution • Contract negotiations • Contract performance measurement • Critical thinking • Cross-functional collaboration • Dashboards • Delivery scheduling • Documentation • Engagement • Financial analysis • Five-phase process • Goal setting • Implementation • Meeting deadlines • Multitasking • Negotiation • Plan development • Problem solving • Product management • Project administration • Project close • Project conception • Project definition • Project execution • Project lifecycle • Project management • Project performance • Project planning • Relationship management • Report writing • Reporting • Risk management • Scheduling • Scrum • Six Sigma • Stakeholder engagement • Strategic planning • Strategy • Supervision • Team management • Time management • Tracking • Training • Verbal communications • Written communications

3.3   Résumé sections

There is no prescribed résumé format that works equally well for everyone. Résumés generally include five or six sections with headings but you can add additional sections to the following typical résumé sections and change the titles of the sections to accurately describe the information presented.

HEADER

List your name, address, e-mail address, and phone number at the top before other sections, similar to this:

JANE DOE
1 Any Street, City, Province/State, Postal/Zip Code
janedoe@anymail.com
(123) 456-7890

OBJECTIVE/VALUE STATEMENT

This is the place to include your personal branding statement from section 1.4.3 or a value statement with keywords from section 3.2.

OBJECTIVE

A senior project manager with over 20 years of experience in delivering innovative, complex, and large-scale IT solutions pursuing a career in leading revolutionizing teams working on cutting-edge designs and technologies in the health sector.

VALUE STATEMENT

A(n) _____ professional with extensive experience in _____, _____, and _____. Key competencies include _____, _____, _____, _____, and _____. Proven success in _____, _____, and _____. Recognized as a subject matter expert in _____, _____, _____, and _____.

SKILLS/AREAS OF EXPERTISE

Refer to section 3.5 and list the relevant competencies you want to highlight from section 1.4.2.4 here.

AREAS OF EXPERTISE

- Expert _____.
- Proficient in _____.
- Exemplary _____.
- Excellent _____.

Alternatively, include up to 12 keywords from your list in section 3.2. Reuse some of the keywords in the Value Statement if needed.

AREAS OF EXPERTISE

- Keyword 1
- Keyword 2
- Keyword 3
- Keyword 4
- Keyword 5
- Keyword 6

WORK EXPERIENCE/HISTORY

Often a job advertisement outlines the duties that the hired person will be doing and the qualifications needed that generally tied to the duties. Read the job advertisement carefully as almost everything you are evaluated on is in the advertisement. Besides showing as much as possible that you have done the same or similar work as the duties listed, show how your competencies would meet each of the requirements/qualifications identified.

For illustration purpose, I am going to use the following job advertisement to demonstrate how to use the CAST method to build this section:

IT PROJECT MANAGER

Responsibilities
- Meet with clients to elicit and clarify specific requirements of each project.
- Coordinate internal and external resource allocation.
- Develop project objectives, scopes, and plans.
- Manage changes in project scope, schedule and costs and make adjustments to project constraints to ensure all projects are delivered on-time, within scope, and within budget.
- Perform risk management to minimize project risks.
- Create and maintain comprehensive project documentation.
- Report and escalate to management as needed.
- Establish and maintain relationships with the client, stakeholders, and third parties/vendors.
- Measure project performance using appropriate systems, tools and techniques.

Qualifications
- PMP certification is a must.
- Solid technical background, with understanding or hands-on experience in software development and web technologies.
- Proven working experience as a project manager in the information technology sector.
- Advanced time management and analytical skills.
- Excellent written and verbal communication skills.
- Strong working knowledge of Microsoft Office.

Use the following worksheet and instructions to gather the information required for your résumé.

1. In the **Job Requirements** column list the qualification statements from the job ad.

2. In the **Refs** column, refer to the competency wheel in section 1.4.1.4 and list the applicable competencies for each job requirement.

3. In the **My Qualifications** column, refer to the appropriate competencies in section 1.4.2.5 and list up to three qualification statements that are relevant and best address each of the requirements. Don't include anything farther back than 15 years unless it is relevant. If applicable, go through the responsibilities section of the job ad and list those statements here (see the bolded statement in the sample below) and also add them to your qualification statements in section 1.4.2.5.

This exercise highlights your fit to a job's specific requirements. It also helps you to discover whether you are qualified for a particular role so that you could avoid wasting time applying for jobs that are not a good fit for you.

Refs	Job Requirements	My Qualifications
C1	PMP certification is a must.	Attained PMP certification since 2006.
C1	Solid technical background, with understanding or hands-on experience in software development and web technologies.	Applied software development and web technologies knowledge to develop IT solutions for international clients.
C1	Proven working experience as a project manager in the information technology sector.	Delivered various innovative, complex, and large-scale IT projects to increase efficiencies and/or savings.
C13 C14	Advanced time management and analytical skills.	Managed multiple simultaneous projects with tight timelines and budgets. Assessed trends in web technologies and developed recommendations for solutions that expanded customer offerings.
C10 C11 C16	Excellent written and verbal communication skills.	Obtained $1M funding approval by presenting a business case with analyses and replacement options for the current case management systems to managers, executives, and sponsors. Introduced the new case management system to staff through a technical guide which resulted in a 20% reduction in support calls. **Met with clients to elicit and clarify specific requirements of each project.**
C12	Strong working knowledge of Microsoft Office.	Certified Microsoft Office Specialist on Microsoft Office 2016.

To convince prospective employers of your relevant experience you must package yourself the way they want. Make it obvious that you meet the selection criteria. For example, if the employer is looking for someone who has HTML skills, your résumé should explicitly mention that you have HTML skills. Don't just say you have been a web developer for years and expect the employer to assume that you have HTML skills. Don't lie or exaggerate your experience, but make sure to highlight the right experience to get you the right job. For example, when you want to get into communications, emphasize the competencies relating to communication.

Whatever you say about yourself in your cover letter and résumé, you must be able to back up with actual skills and experiences. Match your skills and experiences to where you will be working and the type of work you'll be doing. The more the potential employer knows that you've used these skills for similar types of work or to solve similar problems to the ones they have, the better you'll score. For example, if a marketing company is looking for someone with project management experience, a person with any project management experience will score better than someone who has none. A person who has managed marketing projects will score better than someone who managed web development projects.

List paid and unpaid positions you held, name of the organization, city and province/state of its location, and month and year of your employment/involvement. If applicable, include a link to your portfolio if you have examples of your work online.

Using the information from the worksheet above, the following are samples for chronological and functional formats respectively. The Employment History section in the functional format is optional.

WORK EXPERIENCE

ABC Company – City, Province/State – January 2010 to Present

- Attained PMP certification since 2006.
- Applied software development and web technologies knowledge to develop IT solutions for international clients.
- Delivered various innovative, complex, and large-scale IT projects to increase efficiencies and/or savings.
- Managed multiple simultaneous projects with tight timelines and budgets.
- Assessed trends in web technologies and developed recommendations for solutions that expanded customer offerings.
- Obtained $1M funding approval by presenting a business case with analyses and replacement options for the current case management systems to managers, executives, and sponsors.
- Introduced the new case management system to staff through a technical guide which resulted in a 20% reduction in support calls.
- Met with clients to elicit and clarify specific requirements of each project.
- Certified Microsoft Office Specialist on Microsoft Office 2016.

WORK EXPERIENCE

- Attained PMP certification since 2006.
- Applied software development and web technologies knowledge to develop IT solutions for international clients.
- Delivered various innovative, complex, and large-scale IT projects to increase efficiencies and/or savings.
- Managed multiple simultaneous projects with tight timelines and budgets.
- Assessed trends in web technologies and developed recommendations for solutions that expanded customer offerings.
- Obtained $1M funding approval by presenting a business case with analyses and replacement options for the current case management systems to managers, executives, and sponsors.
- Introduced the new case management system to staff through a technical guide which resulted in a 20% reduction in support calls.
- Met with clients to elicit and clarify specific requirements of each project.
- Certified Microsoft Office Specialist on Microsoft Office 2016.

EMPLOYMENT HISTORY
- ABC Company, City, Province/State – January 2010 to Present
- XYZ Company, City, Province/State – January 2001 to December 2010

When the job ad groups qualifications with subheadings, use the same subheading names and list the competencies in the same order.

WORK EXPERIENCE

TECHNICAL COMPETENCY
- Attained PMP certification since 2006.
- Applied software development and web technologies knowledge to develop IT solutions for international clients.
- Delivered various innovative, complex, and large-scale IT projects to increase efficiencies and/or savings.
- Managed multiple simultaneous projects with tight timelines and budgets.
- Assessed trends in web technologies and developed recommendations for

solutions that expanded customer offerings.
- Certified Microsoft Office Specialist on Microsoft Office 2016.

COMMUNICATION SKILLS
- Obtained $1M funding approval by presenting a business case with analyses and replacement options for the current case management systems to managers, executives, and sponsors.
- Introduced the new case management system to staff through a technical guide which resulted in a 20% reduction in support calls.
- Met with clients to elicit and clarify specific requirements of each project.

EMPLOYMENT HISTORY
- ABC Company, City, Province/State – January 2010 to Present
- XYZ Company, City, Province/State – January 2001 to December 2010

TOOLS & SOFTWARE USED

List the tools and software you used in section 1.4.2.1 if it is not already included in other sections of the résumé.

TOOLS & SOFTWARE SKILLS

- Microsoft Word
- Microsoft Outlook
- Adobe InDesign

EDUCATION/TRAINING/COURSES

List institutions attended, including study abroad experience; degrees and dates received; major and concentration; and honours thesis title, if applicable.

List only relevant training and courses. For example, if you are seeking work as a computer programmer, include only computer-related courses.

EDUCATION

Certificate in IT Project Management (PMP) (2006)
XYZ University, City, Province/State

B.S. Business Management (2000 – 2004)
ABC University, City, Province/State
Dean's List

COURSES

2016 – Lean IT
2015 – ITIL Foundation

HONOURS AND AWARDS

Include Dean's List, honour societies, academic awards, scholarships, and relevant professional awards. Incorporate in the Education section if you only have one or two entries.

AWARDS

Dean's List 2000-2004, with 4.0 GPA. Received Student of the Year award in 2004 at ABC University.

ACTIVITIES AND INTERESTS

If you want to include this section, list only activities and interests that pertain to your career goal. Avoid including religious activities or those representing extreme political views.

ACTIVITIES & INTERESTS

- Member of the ABC web development conference.
- **Interests:** Team sports, travelling, and crosswords.

REFERENCES

As employers often ask for references who can vouch for your abilities before, during, or after an interview, it is acceptable to skip this section as it is expected or include a simple statement such as "Available upon request." in this section.

REFERENCES

Available upon request.

3.4   Cover letter

Some recruiters don't even look at cover letters and some pay close attention to them. Some will use the cover letter to decide if they even want to look at the person's résumé while others would use it for evaluation purposes. Always send a cover letter unless the job listing explicitly says not to send one.

As the goal of your cover letter is to make a case for getting selected for a job interview, you will need to demonstrate a compelling argument that you're a strong candidate for the position.

Take time to write a custom cover letter for each job you apply for. For example, mention specifics about the organization or details about someone you know there. Your cover letter provides an opportunity to highlight how you have applied the skills you list in your résumé. Explain why you want to work there, what you can do for them, and how your skills relate to the criteria listed in the job posting. The more you and your skills match the job description, the higher your chances of getting picked for an interview. You can also use your cover letter to explain something in your résumé. For example, a career shift, relocation, or an extended gap in employment.

Don't offer salary information if the job listing doesn't mention it. If you're asked to include salary requirements or salary history with your application, be truthful and include salary ranges rather than specific amounts. For example, "My salary requirement is in the \$_____ to \$_____ range." or an itemized list of your previous salary ranges.

When you email your cover letter and résumé, either type the cover letter into the body of the email and attach the résumé or integrate the cover letter as the first page of the actual résumé and send it as an attachment.

Make it easy for an employer to notice you by strategically naming your email subject and attachment. Labelling them clearly and purposefully helps you stand out and demonstrates your attention to detail. Use your name, the position title and other descriptors. Descriptors can be one of the mandatory requirements or something you know the employer may use as a selection criteria, such as a location. For example, **Jane_Doe_IT_Project_Manager_PMP**.

3.4.1 Sample cover letter

This is a common cover letter type. To create something similar, use the compiled information in sections 3.3 Work Experience/History and 1.4.2.3:

Your Name
Your Address
Your City, State, Zip Code
Your Phone Number
Your Email

Date

Name
Title
Organization
Address
City, State, Zip Code

Dear _____:

I am interested in the position of _____ (reference #_____) as advertised in _____. I have included a copy of my résumé for your review.

I am currently employed as _____. I believe that the skills and experiences I have gained at this position grants me the ability to help you _____.

As _____, I have developed ____, _____, and ____ skills. For example, one of my main duties is to _____. This duty requires _____, _____, and _____ skills and the ability to _____. I have completed _____ and received an award for _____.

I have also gained extensive experience in _____ field that you state in your job requirements. My experience in the _____ has given me the opportunity to become familiar with _____. Through my work with _____, I have become involved in _____. I am always eager to learn more about ____ and I continually research these topics to become more knowledgeable. I would love to bring this passion for _____ and _____ to your company.

I would welcome the opportunity to discuss your job requirements and my qualifications with you. Thank you in advance for your consideration.

Sincerely,

Signature (handwritten or digital)

Your first and last name

3.4.2 "T" cover letter

You help the hiring manager save time and effort in mapping your qualifications to the job requirements when you provide the "T" cover letter by rehashing certain elements in a résumé. You are basically saying, "I'm exactly what you are looking for, and here is why." If your qualifications truly match the job requirements, sending the "T" cover letter along with your résumé increases your chances of passing through that first step and progressing on to the next step in the hiring process.

This type of cover letter works well with the CAST method. It uses the compiled information in sections 3.3 Work Experience/History and can be formatted like this:

Dear _____:

I am interested in the position of _____ (reference #_____) as advertised in _____. I have included a copy of my résumé for your review.

Below is a comparison of your job requirements and my qualifications.

Job Requirements	My Qualifications
• Requirement 1	• Qualification 1
	• Qualification 2
	• Qualification 3
• Requirement 2	• Qualification 1
	• Qualification 2

I would welcome the opportunity to discuss your job requirements and my qualifications with you. Thank you in advance for your consideration.

Sincerely,

Signature (handwritten or digital)

Your first and last name

Or like this ATS-friendly version:

Dear _____:

I am interested in the position of _____ (reference #_____) as advertised in _____. I have included a copy of my résumé for your review.

Below is a comparison of your job requirements and my qualifications.

Job Requirement: _____
My Qualifications:

- _____
- _____
- _____

Job Requirement: _____
My Qualifications:

- _____
- _____
- _____

I would welcome the opportunity to discuss your job requirements and my qualifications with you. Thank you in advance for your consideration.

Sincerely,

Your first and last name

3.5 Checklists for résumé and cover letter

3.5.1 Checklist: Perfecting my résumé and cover letter

☐ Did I remove references to I, me, my, he/she, him/her, and his/her in my résumé since it should not include pronouns?

☐ Did I leave out political, religious, and personal details such as security number, date of birth, and family members' names?

☐ Did I remove hobbies from my résumé unless it is relevant to the job I am applying for?

☐ Did I include company names, locations, and dates (month and year) of past employment, if applicable?

☐ Did I include an education section on my résumé?

☐ Did I include my contact information?

☐ Does my email address sound professional?

☐ When I send my cover letter by email, did I include my contact information in my signature section instead of listing at the top of the message?

☐ When I send my cover letter by email, did I list my name, the position title, and the descriptors in the subject line?

☐ When I send my application by email, did I name my attachments using my name, the position title and other descriptors?

☐ When I send my cover letter in the body of an email, did I skip the date, and start my email message with the salutation?

☐ Did I use an acceptable salutation such as "Dear Hiring Manager," "To Whom It May Concern," "Dear Human Resources Manager," "Dear Sir or Madam," "Dear Company Name Recruiter," or include the name of a contact person if I have one in my cover letter?

☐ Did I include the job title on my cover letter (and/or résumé) that matches the job advertisement?

☐ Did I use an acceptable closing such as "Sincerely," "Regards," "Yours truly," and "Yours sincerely,"?

☐ Did I physically or digitally sign the cover letter?

☐ Did I remove all extraneous details?

☐ Did I check for typos, spelling mistakes, and grammatical errors in both my résumé and cover letter?

☐ Did I follow instructions provided by the employer?

3.5.2 Checklist: Best practices for ATS

☐ It has been customized for the position being sought.

☐ It meets the employer's submission requirements. For example, the number of pages.

☐ It is saved in an approved format such as DOC, DOCX, or TXT.

☐ It uses simply formatted text of 10-point size or above.

☐ It includes standard fonts such as Arial, Calibri, Georgia, Tahoma, and Verdana.

☐ It does not contain complex formatting (condensed or expanded text). For example, don't use extra spaces between letters, because the ATS can't "read" it.

☐ It does not contain images or graphics.

☐ It does not include any special characters or accented words.

☐ It uses MM/YY, MM/YYYY, or Month YYYY (e.g. 08/19, 08/2019, Aug 2019 or August 2019) for dates.

☐ It does not include any information in the headers or footers of the document when it is saved in Microsoft Word format.

☐ It has been thoroughly edited and spellchecked as the ATS will not recognize misspelled words.

☐ It contains proper capitalization and punctuation. Both can affect how information is parsed and assigned within the ATS database.

☐ Includes clearly defined sections.

☐ It uses the full, spelled-out version of a term in addition to abbreviations and acronyms. For example, Project Manager (PM).

☐ It incorporates relevant, specific, targeted keywords and phrases for the type of position being sought. For example, "PowerPoint" instead of "presentation software".

3.6   References

Although reference checks often happen at the end before an employer decides whether to offer the job to you, it is important to prepare your references at the beginning. Be sure the people you are using as references know they may be contacted so they can help you get the job. Once the reference checks happen, it's out of your control, and now up to others.

Assemble an updated list of contacts that can persuasively communicate your professional attributes and qualifications for the job. You could also use anyone who can endorse your character and abilities. Unless it is a requirement, your references don't have to be your current manager or co-workers, especially if they are not aware you are job searching. If you are asked when you can't give a past or current manager as a reference, provide a good reason, for example, either of you were too new to the position.

Use the following checklist to prepare your references.

3.6.1   Checklist: **Preparing my references**

- ☐ Call ahead to get permission and assess the reference's eagerness to talk and vouch for me.

- ☐ Verify contact information and the reference's communication preferences, for example, what method and best times.

- ☐ Ask them the three words they would choose to describe me to help me project the image I want.

- ☐ If possible, give the reference a list of the jobs I have applied so that they are aware of which employers might be contacting them.

- ☐ If possible, give them a copy of my current résumé or any other information that may help prepare him/her.

☐ If necessary, ask the reference to keep my request confidential.

☐ Offer to be a reference should he/she ever needs it.

☐ Write a thank-note after he/she agreed to serve as my reference.

☐ Inform my reference of the result and write a thank-you note.

Your chances of getting selected for an interview are high when you can show your competencies through your résumé and cover letter. Getting an interview is a step closer to getting a job offer. In the next chapter, let's get into how to prepare for your interview, including how to use your CAR stories from your CAST profile.

4. PREPARING FOR AN INTERVIEW

Hiring is an expensive process and the hiring manager's reputation is on the line every time he/she hires someone. You need to sell yourself as the best person for the job in order to get the job offer. Answer every interview question in a positive and focused way, but don't be afraid to relax a little bit, ask questions, and tell stories when it is appropriate. Your answers should be strategically focused on getting you one step closer to the job offer.

Your job is to help the interviewer visualize the company with you in the role that you are applying for. All your answers should be strategically focused on getting you one step closer to the job offer.

4.1 Portfolio

As part of preparing for an interview, you may want to create a portfolio. A portfolio can include anything that you can use as supporting evidence of your accomplishments: a list of different types of projects you've worked on, a collection of award certificates, and recommendation letters. You may be able to refer to it during an interview or to leave a copy for your interviewers when you depart. Always ask before you use or share it. Even if the interviewer doesn't want to see it or you to use it, having a portfolio helps to show that you are serious and well-prepared.

4.2 Checklist: Interview preparation

Preparation is important because you often don't get a second chance in an interview. Use the following checklist to find out in advance how your interview(s) is/are going to be conducted. The more you know, the better you will be prepared.

☐ How many interviews will I be attending? _____

☐ Where will the interview(s) be held? _____

☐ How many interviewers will there be? _____

☐ How many internal and/or external interviewers will there be? _____

☐ How many onsite and/or remote interviews will there be? _____

☐ Will I or the organization pay for my interview-related expenses? _____

☐ Is this a direct hiring by the organization or by a third party? _____

☐ Will questions be provided in advance or asked at the interview? _____

☐ Will there be more than one interview question? _____

☐ What type(s) of interview questions will be asked? _____

☐ Will the interview be timed? _____

☐ Will the interview be documented? _____

☐ Will there be a test? If so what kind? _____

☐ Will I be expected to make a presentation? If so what are the guidelines? _____

☐ What do I need to bring to the interview? For example, computer, watch, notepad, pen, extra copies of résumé, presentation, references) _____

☐ Do I have my portfolio ready? (optional) _____

☐ Did I prepare my mock interview? This includes anticipating the interview questions, scripting appropriate answers, and practising out loud (with a friend and/or voice/video recording).

☐ Is there anything else I need to prepare for? _____

4.3   Types of interview questions

Below are the explanations for the seven types of interview questions and in the next section, you will learn how to use your CAST profile to prepare answers.

1. Technical questions

2. Behavioural questions

3. General questions

4. Situational questions

5. Unusual questions

6. Difficult or sensitive questions

7.   Inappropriate or illegal questions.

Use the CAR technique (section 1.4.2.6) as a story structure for answers to situational and behavioural interview questions. You can also use it to add a background story for some general and technical questions.

4.3.1   Technical questions

These questions aim at assessing your knowledge of job-specific programs, policies, procedures, tools, systems, and people related to the job. For example, "How would you develop a press release outlining the organization's priorities?", "How do you use a computer?", and "How do you serve a customer?"

Typically, more than half of interviewing time will be spent on these job-specific competencies. You need to know the job in order to do well in the interview.

To score extra points for questions such as, "What are the key…", "What are the most important…", besides identifying them, you need to put the facts in context, how they relate to other things, and the reason why they are important.

Your experience matters, but you won't be hired strictly based on what you've done in the past. In addition to having general knowledge about how to do something, you will need to show that you have two types of technical knowledge:

- Theoretical knowledge about something ("Demonstrated knowledge of agile methodologies" or "Solid technical background in _____").

- Practical knowledge about something specific ("Hands-on experience in software development and web technologies" or ("Knowledge of _____, _____, and _____").

4.3.2 General questions

These questions aim at assessing your personality and obtaining information about your education, work history, skills or knowledge, as they relate to the job you are applying for. Your answer will be assessed and scored based on how well you organize your facts to show that you understand the requirements, have the proper qualifications and are a good fit for the position. For example, "Describe what skills and experiences you possess that make you an ideal candidate?"

Employers want to know if you understand the job and how your skills and experiences will contribute. They also want to know if this job is right for you and that you are going to be satisfied doing it.

4.3.3   Behavioural questions

These questions focus on how you handled various work situations in the past. Your response will reveal your skills, abilities, and personality in how you think and what tools or strategies you use to approach and solve problems. These behaviour questions are specific and challenge you to provide concrete examples. For example, "Tell me about a time when you had to design a solution to a key problem in your project. What did you do, and what was the result?"

Employers want to know if you can and will do your job as you should. They want to know if you can plan, organize, prioritize, and adapt. They want to know if you are a diligent team player who can work independently, produce consistent results, take initiatives, and learn from criticism and mistakes. They also want to understand how you work, how you behave, and how you handle difficult situations, stress, conflicts, and workloads.

4.3.4 Situational questions

Like behavioural questions, situational questions assess analytical and problem-solving skills and the ability to handle daily tasks effectively. You are asked to suggest a solution to a given hypothetical situation that you may be faced with on the job. For example, "You are working on a project that has to be completed by this afternoon and your manager assigns you another task to be completed by tomorrow morning. You know you can't meet both deadlines. What would you do?"

4.3.5 Unusual questions

These questions can be intimidating and can throw you for a loop. They aim to reveal your thought process, personality, and imagination. Through questions like, "What animal would you be if you could be any animal and why?" and "On a scale of one to 10, how lucky are you in life?" employers want to know if you can think through the problem logically using your analytic skills and creativity without getting flustered under pressure. You can't prepare for all these questions and there are usually no right or wrong answers. When possible, tie your answer into the qualities necessary to perform the job well.

Talk your way through the problem and ask any questions that you need to clarify what is being asked.

4.3.6   Difficult or sensitive questions

These questions are the toughest to answer, like "Tell us about a time that you went against corporate directives." or "Why were you fired?" Provide short answers as honestly and positively as possible. Only tell a story if it puts you in a good light.

Employers want to know if you will pose a risk to their organization. They want to know if you are trustworthy, dependable, and flexible for their long-term goals. They want to know if you will be an advocate for the organization and protect its assets and reputation.

Ultimately, you must judge each situation independently. Frame your answer to allay the interviewer's concerns and consider the needs of stakeholders and the consequences.

4.3.7   Inappropriate or illegal questions

Questions about marital status, family status, gender, nationality, religion, or age are illegal, but they still get asked unintentionally without malice. If you are asked and are uncomfortable answering these questions, redirect the conversation back to professional matters. You could say something like, "I am not sure if that is relevant, but I'm very interested in learning about the potential for professional growth here. Can you tell me more about that?"

4.4   Using CAST to prepare for an interview

Many common interview questions fall into more than one type and cover different competencies. For example, a hiring manager may ask a behaviour question about your technical skills, such as "Tell me about a time when you had to troubleshoot a technical problem. What steps did you follow? How did you verify that you were correct?" that cover these competencies: C1-Technical capability, C2-Equipment and program knowledge, C14-Analytical thinking, C15-Problem solving, and C21-Commitment.

Continuing with the job advertisement in section 3.3 under **Work Experience/History**, this section demonstrates how to use the CAST method to prepare for your interview.

Use the following worksheet and instructions to gather and organize the information:

1. In the **Job Responsibilities** column list the responsibilities statements from the job ad.

2. In the **Refs** column, refer to the competency wheel in section 1.4.1.4 and list the applicable key competencies for each responsibility.

Refs	Job Responsibilities
C10, C11	Meet with clients to elicit and clarify specific requirements of each project.
C8, C19	Coordinate internal and external resource allocation.
C1	Develop project objectives, scopes, and plans.
C1, C2, C8, C13, C17, C19, C25	Manage changes in project scope, schedule and costs and make adjustments to project constraints to ensure all projects are delivered on-time, within scope, and within budget.
C1, C5, C14	Perform risk management to minimize project risks.
C11, C16	Create and maintain comprehensive project documentation.
C16	Report and escalate to management as needed.
C23	Establish and maintain relationships with the client, stakeholders, and third parties/vendors.
C1, C12	Measure project performance using appropriate systems, tools and techniques.

3. List the competencies in the **Refs** column in ascending order then remove all duplicates so you'd end up with a list like this: C1, C2, C5, C8, C10, C11, C12, C13, C14, C16, C17, C19, C23, C25.

4. Refer to the following table and review the sections that correspond to the competencies on your list. So for the list in #3 above, you'd review sections 1.4.2.1a, 1.4.2.5, 1.4.2.6, 4.6.1 and 4.6.2.

Refs	Review Sections
C1 to 12	1.4.2.1a, 1.4.2.5 and 4.6.1
C13 to 25	1.4.2.5, 1.4.2.6, 4.6.1, and 4.6.2
C26 to C28	1.4.2.5, 1.4.2.6, and 4.6.3

While some hiring managers provide interview questions in advance of the interview, often you can't predict the questions that will be asked. Preparing for an interview doesn't mean that you need to memorize interview answers. Instead, try to anticipate interview questions. The exercise above helps you focus on the most likely questions. And since you know all your qualifications and stories, who is better at telling them than you are?

4.5   ABC Principles

No matter how prepared you are you can't prepare for every possible question. Furthermore, there is no one answer that is right for every job. It's easy to make mistakes in interviews. Don't beat yourself up if you can't answer or stumble to find the right one. Picture the competency wheel in section 1.4.1.4 and before answering each question, ask yourself: **What is this question about?** Focus your answer on your qualifications if it is about something that requires an action. Focus on your involvement with people if it is about interactions, settings, or emotions. Focus on yourself if it is about traits or values.

If you still can't answer then say something like, "It's an interesting/a thought-provoking question. I'd like to think it though. May I get back to you on that?"

Always frame your answers around the following ABC principles:

- **Make it <u>A</u>ligned with the job.** How can I make my personality, background, experience, or skill set meet or exceed the requirements of this job? How can I take what I did or what I have and match it up with the requirements of this job?

- **Make it the <u>B</u>est.** How can I focus on the positives? How can I show that I've learned something without complaining or badmouthing anyone?

- **Make it about the <u>C</u>ompany.** How can I tell the interviewer what he/she wants to know? How can I show my understanding of what the company cares about?

4.6   Interview questions

Competency-based interviews are an increasing trend. Every interview is set up with a structured set of questions and it is conducted the same for every candidate to measure how a candidate meets the job requirements and if he/she has the knowledge and skill set to be successful.

The interview may begin with open-ended questions about the field in general, including current events within the field. Besides getting a sense of your professional attitude and viewpoint, these questions help the hiring manager gauge your background knowledge of and interest in the field.

To help determine what you know and how strong your technical competencies are, the hiring manager may ask direct questions about technical facts and data related to the job. He/she may ask you to read a technical diagram, interpret a chart or report or identify components on a schematic.

When there is a practical component to the job, a hiring manager may ask for a description of how to perform certain functions. He/she may ask behavioural or situational questions to gain insight into how you have applied or would apply your technical skills to address a situation or solve a problem.

In addition to asking questions, the hiring manager may ask you to solve a given problem within a time limit on a computer or talk through how you would solve it. Sometimes it is equally important that you provide the right answer and also your approach to the problem and solving it.

In some jobs, tests may include role-playing and completing personality tests. If you are asked to partner with other candidates, your interactions and attitude will also be scored.

You may be asked to do a presentation which will be evaluated based on content and your presentation skills. Ask how much time you'd have and invest the time and effort to create a presentation deck or handout. Make sure to rehearse it within the time limit.

Below are some interview questions with tips and prompts for answers.

4.6.1 Can you <u>do</u> the job?

4.6.1.1 Accomplishments

What are you most proud of? • Tell me about an accomplishment you are most proud of.

Select from section 1.4.2.5 those work-related and job-relevant awards, accomplishments, and successes that would be especially impressive to this company and the position you are applying for. It is an opportunity for you to brag and quantify your accomplishments as much as you can.

If you are asked to highlight one specific accomplishment in greater depth, back up your claims with significant details about the challenges and obstacles you overcame and hard data about the impact you had at your company, such as how much time and resources you saved or revenue you made.

This is also your chance to brag by pulling from your portfolio (section 4.1) to show the note you received for a job well done from a client or your manager.

Answer prompts

I am most proud of how I improved _____. I managed to overcome _____,

_____, and _____. *I contribute this achievement to my* _____, _____, *and*

_____ *skills. I am proud of this achievement because* _____. *It felt* _____ *to*

see   my   _____   *put   to   good   use.   I   received* _____   *as*

recognition/acknowledgement for my contribution. It taught me that with

_____ *I can reach all of my goals.*

4.6.1.2 Creativity

Give me an example of your creativity.

Most employers value creativity in the workplace as they gain a competitive edge through being innovative and forward-thinking in their approach to business.

The example isn't about arts unless you work in a creative field; it is about how you creatively solved a problem at work or brought about positive change or innovation that led to increased productivity or revenue.

Refer to sections 1.4.2.5 and 1.4.2.6 (C15) to quantify or back up your example of creativity and to show how you've added value. The example should be relevant to the work you do. Provide details that paint a vivid picture of what you've accomplished that led to innovations or had a significant impact on the organization.

Answer prompts

One of my key creative accomplishments occurred in _____ when I had to _____. I _____, _____, and _____. I am most proud of how I improved _____ because _____. I contribute this achievement to my _____, _____, and _____ skills. It felt _____ to see how my _____ contribute to _____.

4.6.1.3 Duties and responsibilities

What were the responsibilities of your last position?

The hiring manager wants to understand your perception of your last job and to confirm the job title on your résumé matches up with the actual work you did.

Select three or four responsibilities from section 1.4.2.5 and start with either the biggest responsibility you had or the one that is most relevant to the job you are interviewing for. Demonstrate that you are a great fit for this job because you've been successful at doing similar things in the past and you can do the same here.

Answer prompts

In my last position, I was responsible for _____. That required _____, _____, and _____. I was able to _____. I really like this type of work because _____.

What will you miss about your present/last job?

The hiring manager wants to see how your past job can help you succeed in the position you are applying to. Think about how to take general tasks from your current or previous job and apply them to the tasks you might have at this new job. For example, if you've been working with shoppers in a retail job and this new technical job includes working with clients, you could say that you've loved building relationships with your customers. Or, if the new position includes a lot of data organization and reporting, you can talk about how you loved organizational tasks at a previous job.

Answer prompts

At my previous job, I was able to _____. *I was given opportunities to* _____ *and use my* _____, _____, *and* _____ *skills. I love being able to* _____ *because* _____. *I am very excited to get the same opportunities here.*

4.6.1.4 Education and experiences

Discuss your educational background. • What can you offer us that someone else cannot? • What aspects of your background have been the most helpful? • Why should I consider/hire you for this position? • What makes you qualified for this position? • Tell me about yourself. • How did you prepare for this work? • How would you describe yourself?

These questions are not about your hobbies, personal details, or a full employment history. Your answer is your pitch on why you're the right person for the job. Speak about your education and experiences that matter to the organization. Talk through the top three most important achievements. Show instances in the past where you've made or saved company money and talk about how those relevant accomplishments and experiences qualify you for this role. Tailor your answer to what you think are the reasons the hiring manager wants to hire you. You want him/her to know that you are skilled, you have accomplished some great things, and you can bring those abilities and accomplishments to work for him/her.

Sometimes it's a blend of the different pieces of your education, experiences, skill sets, and personality that makes you unique and desirable. Think about how and why your uniqueness

makes you valuable, such as:

- The qualifications or skills you have that are hard to find.

- The things you do better than most of your peers.

- The valuable things that your co-workers and managers say about you.

- The thing that you are best at, or the first, or the only one.

- An important area in which you are exceptionally knowledgeable.

- The part of your job you are most passionate about.

- Your exceptional record of promotions or career growth.

- Your most impressive professional accomplishment of the past five years.

- You have more than usual education, training, or certifications.

- You have won awards or been formally recognized for superior work.

Answer prompts

With my degree/certification in _____, I spent _____ years in _____ where I _____. Some of my achievements include _____, _____, and _____ are due to my _____, _____, and _____ skills. I am eager to show you what I can do here.

What interests you most about this position?

The hiring manager wants to know that you are interested in this job specifically, that you understand the job description, and that you are applying because you have qualities and experience relevant to this position. Be enthusiastic and positive. Emphasize key points in the job description and mention those specific keywords and phrases that appealed to you. Bring up values and characteristics of the company that parallel your own traits and values. Highlight what you bring to the table. The company wants to know how your skills will add to the company, not how having the job will improve your situation.

Answer prompts

What interested me most about this position was _____. I have always had a keen interest in _____. In this position, I can use _____ to _____ for the organization.

Are you overqualified for this position?

If you are overqualified for the job, employers want to find out if you'll be happy and productive in this position in their organization. You will need to ease their concerns that:

- You are desperate for a job

- You will be bored or unhappy

- This job is just a stepping stone for you.

Except for money and responsibilities, talk about certain aspects of this job and how they fulfill your goals and desires. Provide reasons why you got into this line of work and tie it into why this job is such a good fit for you.

Answer prompts

Because I love _____, _____, and _____, that's why I choose _____ area/field as a career. I am excited about this job because I've learned about how the company handle _____, _____, and _____. This job fits me because of _____, _____, and _____.

Why should we hire you when you lack the experience we are looking for?

This question is asked when the hiring manager is somewhat interested in you but is a bit concerned about your lack of experience.

Answer prompts

I understand your concern about my lack of experience but I am a quick learner and am willing to do anything it takes to get up to speed. I have kept up my knowledge through _____ on _____. I am eager to use my skills in _____, _____, and _____ to bring the results you want.

How did you hear about this position?

If you learned of the position through someone who has a connection, talk about why he/she thinks your skills and experiences make you ideal for this position.

If you learned of the position through an advertisement, event or article, explain what it was about the position that caught your eye. In all cases, tell the hiring manager why you're the perfect candidate to fill the role.

Answer prompts

I love _____ and I am passionate about _____. I have been looking for opportunities to use my _____, _____, and _____ skills so when I learned about this job through _____, I really want to be a part of the team.

4.6.1.5 Managing workload and timelines

How do you handle your workload? • Are you good at delegating tasks?

Select from section 1.4.2.6 (C13) a story that reflects your experience or talk about how you prioritize, ask for help, or delegate.

Answer prompts

I have experience dealing with heavy workloads. I found that the best thing to do is to _____ to help me gain control and reduce stress. I also use _____ to help me manage my workload and timelines. Sometimes I would speak to my manager to _____. Sometimes I would delegate some tasks to the right people to give them a chance to _____.

How many hours in a week do you normally work?

Depending on the position you are applying for, the hiring manager might want to know if you are effective in time management or that you are willing to work extra hours as needed. You want to show that you have an excellent work ethic and you will do what needs to be done to make the company successful. Describe how you complete your work and highlight your time management skills and overall effectiveness in a typical workweek. Mention the high quality of your past work and your desire to continue being efficient. Incorporate any special qualities such as persistence, tenacity or focus.

Answer prompts

- *Select a story from section 1.4.2.6 (C13-Time management).*

- *I work hard each day and with my _____, _____, and skills, I can effectively complete all my tasks during the week. I am proud of my ability to consistently deliver high quality work. When there are more important or difficult projects, I am willing to _____.*

4.6.1.6 Solving problems

What major problem have you encountered and how did you deal with it? • Tell me how you handled a difficult situation/assignment. • What assignment was difficult and how did you resolve the issue? • Tell me about a time when you had to solve a problem but didn't have all the necessary information about it at hand.

Solving problems is a common skill that many employers look for in their employees. In every sector, problems are inevitable and will arise in one form or another. When problems occur, employees are expected to use their initiative and develop suitable solutions to alleviate or eliminate them. Often many competencies are required in solving problems, for example:

- Identify and diagnose issues (C1-Technical capability and C2-Equipment and program knowledge).

- Organize and analyze (C5-Data analysis) accurate and complete information (C4-Research).

- Recognize key or underlying issues and trends (C6-Identify patterns or connections), evaluate options (C14-

Analytical thinking), and develop contingency plans (C8-Planning).

- Create new concept models or to devise ways to overcome obstacles (C15-Resourcefulness).

- Coordinate (C23-Collaboration) with subject-matter experts to interpret policies (C7-Policies) and regulations (C27-Compliance).

- Exercise business judgement to determine opportunities and risks (C9-Business acumen) and make decisions in a timely manner (C20-Decision making) after considering the impact on quality (C21-Commitment), ethical conducts (C26-Responsibility and ethics) and other relevant aspects.

- Communicate (C16-Communication) through speaking, listening (C10-Speaking and Listening), and writing (C11-Writing) to address key concerns (C17-Negotiate), to gain approval from senior management for implementing the solution (C19-Persuasion), and to manage change (C25-Change management).

- Manage workload (C13-Time management) and handle pressures (C24-Handling pressures and stress) while regulating emotions (C22-Interpersonal awareness) to ensure objectives are met.

- Use different technological tools to assist the process (C12-Computer literacy).

Answer prompts

Select a story from section 1.4.2.6 (C19-Problem solving) to describe how you would plan, approach, evaluate, and analyze before you decide on which action to take. Mention as many skills, especially a communication skill, you used to resolve the issue.

4.6.1.7 Strengths and weaknesses

What do you consider to be your greatest strengths and weaknesses?

Talk in detail about your accomplishments, skills, and experiences for strengths. Mention responsibilities you had that correlate to the role you are applying for.

For weaknesses, provide examples that show you understand where you struggle in a professional setting and what you are currently doing to improve that weakness. Pick a weakness that is not relevant to the job you are applying for or likely to cause any performance issues. For example, if you are applying for a technical job and public speaking isn't your strong suit, perhaps you've joined Toastmasters to sharpen your skills. You can also use a strength that you could improve on as your disadvantage.

Answer prompts

I believe my degree/certification in _____ and experience in working in the _____ field are part of my strengths. I also consider my strengths to be _____, _____, and _____. I am proud of these strengths that have proven beneficial to the companies I worked for. I spend _____ years as _____ and I achieved _____, _____, and _____. _____ is not my strongest suit, and I've _____, _____, and _____ to improve it.

4.6.2 Can you <u>fit in</u>?

4.6.2.1 Feedback

Tell me about a time when you had to give some difficult feedback.

Giving negative feedback can be a sensitive matter and requires good communication skills to do it well. Employers want to know if you can approach negative subjects in a positive manner with forethought and sensitivity. Your answer needs to demonstrate that you understand the nuances and sensitivity of the situation by thinking about things like:

- How the person will react.

- The impact of your feedback on the person.

- What you want him/her to do with your feedback once he/she has it.

- The outcome you want and what you need to say or do to get that outcome.

- The long-term effect you want.

- How you want everyone to move forward from here.

Answer prompts

Use your CAR story S23.4 in section 1.4.2.6 (C23-Collaboration).

4.6.2.2 Hobbies

What are your hobbies/outside interests?

Employers want to know if you are a good cultural fit for their organization. Talk about hobbies that most people can identify with and those that make you look energetic or intelligent.

Answer prompts

- *Outdoor activities such as running, hiking, and walking.*

- *Personal interests such as traveling and trying new things.*

- *Education activities such as reading and taking classes.*

4.6.2.3 Pressure and stress

How do you work under pressure?

Pressure can be viewed as a positive motivator while stress is negative and harmful when it occurs too often. When you are asked where you can work under pressure, the employer wants to hear about an example of a time you were under pressure and rose to the occasion to complete a task or solve a problem. He/she wants to be reassured that when things get tough, you will not crack under the weight of all your responsibilities.

Recognize the fact that pressure is in fact a part of the job, then bring up relevant skills and experiences you used when you were under pressure (not because of your own actions) to successfully finish something. Talk about how pressure makes you a better worker.

Answer prompts

Use one of your CAR stories in section 1.4.2.6 (C24-Handling pressure and stress).

4.6.2.4 Resolving conflicts

Have you ever had difficulty with a supervisor? How did you resolve the conflict? • Tell me about a time when you disagreed with your supervisor/manager.

This question is about how you deal with conflicts and confrontation and how you come up with solutions. The hiring manager wants to know if you can work well with others, be professional, and productive. He/she wants to see that you can be empathetic and that you are willing and able to negotiate in a peaceful manner. Show that you are a professional who contributes alternative workable solutions to a disagreement or conflict.

If you never experienced dealing with a difficult supervisor or manager, say so. Otherwise, show the positive and happy ending version without badmouthing him/her.

Answer prompts

Use your CAR story S23.1 in section 1.4.2.6 (C23-Collaboration).

How have you responded to a colleague who has put you down? • Have you ever been on a team where someone was not pulling their own weight? How did you handle it?

If you don't have either experience, say "I'm glad that I haven't had that happen."

If you have dealt with a colleague who has put you down, tell a story that shows you are a capable professional with good judgement who can handle difficult situations on your own and get to a positive outcome.

Answer prompts

Use your CAR story S23.6 in section 1.4.2.6 (C23-Collaboration).

If someone from your team didn't contribute, tell the story and focus on what you are supposed to be working on to get the job done without badmouthing anyone.

Answer prompts

Use your CAR story S23.8 in section 1.4.2.6 (C23-Collaboration).

4.6.2.5 Team work

How are work teams or groups organized?

The hiring manager wants to see what you are used to and if you can adapt to the company's work environment.

Focus on the positives of working with a team or group and the relevant experiences and tasks. Highlight your responsibilities within the team or group and mention how effective you were with your coworkers.

Answer prompts

In my last _____ position, we split teams in a way that would allow everyone to _____ and _____. I was responsible for _____, _____, and _____. It was a positive experience because _____.

Have you considered starting your own business?

A hiring manager is trying to gain insights into your personal views and characteristics. He/she wants to know if you are a team player who fits into the position you are interviewing for and can support the organization's interests and find satisfaction in working as an employee. Demonstrate that you would make a reliable and committed employee. Explain your desired career path, emphasize why your skills are ideally suited for work as an employee, and describe the factors that make working for the company the ideal option for you. Mention also that you intend to continue working as an employee.

Answer prompts

I think my skills are best suited to a career in _____. I know that a position with an employer will let me focus on developing _____, _____, and _____ skills and help me reach my goal of becoming _____. I enjoy working in positions where I can _____ and be a _____ employee.

4.6.2.6 Work style

How would you describe your work style?

Say that you are comfortable working alone or as a team member and whether you need lots of details or minimal direction. Describe your best qualities that fit well with the job you want. If the job typically involves you working alone, then say that part first. You can also ask how much time the job position is spent working alone and working with a team.

Answer prompts

As I am self-motivated and can work with minimal direction. I like that when I work alone, I can _____ and _____. I also enjoy working in a team environment because as a team member, I can use my _____, _____, and _____ to help us succeed.

Describe the best manager you've ever had. • *Describe your supervisor's management style.*

The hiring manager is trying to see how you assess work situations and whether or not you would be able to thrive under the organization's management style.

Show your versatility and ability to work with various types of people. Find a way to highlight particular characteristics that helped you succeed under your supervisor or generalize positive traits from more than one supervisor/manager. If you are aware of the management style of the company, focus on your experience with a supervisor that used that same style.

Keep your answer neutral and generic in a positive tone. For example, good communication skills, leadership skills, a sense of humour, knowledge, fairness, and loyalty are good traits for managers to have.

Answer prompts

In general, I have had the opportunity to work with excellent managers. I have always been able to _____ and they would often _____. However, if I would have to choose one I would say _____ because _____. I believe good managers are those who _____, _____, and give me opportunities to contribute to the organization.

4.6.3   Can you be trusted?

4.6.3.1 Authority

How would you feel about working for someone who knows less than you?

The hiring manager wants to know if you are willing to learn and accept authority from people who know less or younger than you.

Answer prompts

I enjoy learning and I found that I can always learn something useful from anyone even though they may know less than me in one area but more in another one.

What would you do if you don't get this position?

When you are applying for a position in your current organization and are asked what you would do if you don't get it, the hiring manager wants to know if you are a team player who is interested in the good of the organization and not just in your own career advancement.

Answer prompts

Even though I believe I'm a great fit for this role because of _____, _____, and _____, I will support whoever gets this position. I will keep doing the great job I always do and work towards an advancement in this company.

4.6.3.2   Career path

Why did you choose this career? • What is your ideal job?

Concentrate on what you are going to learn and get from this job. Your answer should demonstrate that you are someone who:

- Has a vision.

- Can set realistic goals and plans that align with the position, your skills, experience, and interests.

- Is committed.

Explain why you made the career decisions in the past, and how your new direction is a better fit for you. You can also highlight the ways in which your previous experience is relatable and transferrable to your new potential role, making you a more versatile candidate who may be able to bring a fresh perspective to the organization.

Answer prompts

I chose this career because I love _____. I noticed that the job posting lists _____, _____, and _____ as the essential job functions. I have always enjoyed _____ and _____ so after I started _____, I became interested in _____. I developed _____, _____, and skills and I yearned to learn more so I focused on _____. As I further developed my abilities I decided to pursue a career in the field of _____. I'm now looking for a job where I can apply the _____, _____, and _____ skills I already have and develop new ones too.

Why are you leaving your current job?

Be honest and positive and never bash your past employers. Respond that you're eager to take on new opportunities. Explain why and how this role and company is a better fit than previous positions. It's truthful and a perfectly acceptable answer if you were let go or were laid off. If you were fired, share what you've learned from the experience, how you've grown, and how the experience will shape how you will tackle your new job, like: "I really enjoyed my work at _____ and gained valuable experience from working there. I was able to _____, _____, and _____. I developed _____ but unfortunately, things didn't work out because _____. I learned that to do _____, I need to _____, so I _____. I know I'll put that knowledge to use. That is what attracted me to your company because you value _____."

Answer prompts

- *I loved my company and my job but the opportunities for advancement are limited and I would like to expand my knowledge in this field by using my skills in _____, _____, and _____.*

- *I want to work for a company where I can _____ and I know I can apply the _____, _____, and _____ skills I've developed to this job.*

- *I have been doing the job for _____ number of years now and feel I am ready and can contribute more to a new challenge with more responsibility.*

- *I am interested in a new challenge and an opportunity to use my skills and experience in a different capacity than I have in the past and my current employer has no opportunities in the direction I'd like to head.*

- *I was laid off from my last position when our department was eliminated due to corporate restructuring/merger.*

- *I'm relocating to this area due to family circumstances and left my previous position to make the move.*

- *I recently received my degree, and I want to utilize my educational background in my next position.*

- *I left my last position to spend more time with my family. Now that circumstances have changed, I'm ready for employment again.*

- *I was commuting to the city and spending a significant amount of time each day on travel. I would prefer to be closer to home.*

- *Honestly, I wasn't considering a move until I saw this job posting and I was intrigued by the position and the company. It sounds like an exciting opportunity and an ideal match with my qualifications.*

What are your (long range) career goals? • Where do you see yourself five years from now?

The hiring manager wants to determine if you are likely to stay with the company in the future. Show him/her that you have put some thought into your professional career. Briefly touch on short-term goals if you haven't had the chance to address them. Focus on your overall career path and highlight your realistic ambition to develop professionally.

Answer prompts

I am driven to be the best at what I do. My goal right now is to find a position at a company where I can _____, _____, and _____. I love to have opportunities to _____, _____, and work with people I can really learn from. Eventually, I'd like to assume more _____ responsibilities and get involved in _____.

Why was there a gap in your employment? • What have you been doing since you got laid off?

The hiring manager wants to know if you can stay active and positive, be productive, and able to keep going and find solutions in a difficult situation.

Address the issue directly and honestly. Share what you've been doing during your unemployment (for example, volunteering, taking classes, pursuing certifications, writing, speaking, blogging) and explain how and why those activities will benefit you in your new role.

Answer prompts

During that time, I _____ to _____. I wanted to _____. I've learned

_____, _____, and _____. *I feel the experience and knowledge I gained was* _____ *and will help me perform better in this job.*

4.6.3.3   Commitment

Are you willing to travel? • How do you feel about working nights and weekends? • Would you work on holidays/weekends? • Would you work over 40 hours a week?

These questions are intended to gauge your openness to do what it takes to fulfill your job responsibilities as needed. Provide an answer that describes your understanding of the requirement for the job and emphasize that you are committed to fulfilling your job responsibilities.

Answer prompts

I know this job will require _____ *because* _____. *I have always been able to complete my tasks within* _____. *I understand that* _____ *may be required sometimes. I work efficiently, but when it is needed, I will gladly oblige. I am happy to occasionally* _____.

Is there anything that will prevent you from getting to work on time?

The hiring manager wants to know if you are reliable and that you have put just as much thought into how you will be able to fulfill the commitment of being on time.

Answer prompts

I will not have any issues getting to work on time. I pride myself in being on time so I make sure _____. Though I do plan to utilize _____, if anything were to change I can _____, _____, or _____ to get to work.

Are you willing to relocate?

Whether you are willing to relocate or not, confirm that the job is important to you without committing.

Answer prompts

- *I am not at a point in my life where I can make a major move. However, I am confident that I can provide complete dedication to this position right now and use my skills in _____, _____, and _____. I do not necessarily want to stay in this city forever, so I may be able to relocate in the future.*

- *I'm interested in advancing my career and this job is a great fit because it allows me to use my skills in _____, _____, and _____. I'd consider relocation if it's necessary.*

4.6.3.4 Company research

Tell me something about our company. • What can you tell us about our company? • What is the company's mission statement? • What is the company's relationship with its customers? • What interests you about our products? • Who are our competitors? • Why do customers choose this company? • What is your ideal company?

The hiring manager wants to know whether you've done any company research, care about the organization, and will be an ambassador for it. Show that you are knowledgeable about the organization and where it's going by mentioning its strategies, initiatives, mission and values using a few keywords and phrases from the company's website. Talk about how you would fit in and contribute to its culture. Share a personal example or two. For example, if you're interviewing for a position at a hospital, talk about the fund-raising activities you participated in or your passion for volunteering your time to help people in hospices.

Answer prompts

I'm personally drawn to this mission because _____. I am very excited about working here because I know _____, _____, and _____ about the company. I think I'm a good fit because of _____, _____, and _____.

4.6.3.5 Compliance and standards

Tell us about a time that you went against corporate directives. Why? How did it turn out?

If you are asked about a time you went against corporate directives, you probably don't want to answer in the affirmative because it may paint you in a negative light to your interviewer. Unless you have an incident that can put you in positive light or the company values maverick spirits, don't volunteer information.

Answer prompts

I believe it is important to comply with corporate directives and I've never gone against corporate directives. Is that an action that is encouraged here?

Can you give an example of a time when you had to conform to a policy with which you disagree?

If you have conformed to a policy with which you disagreed, explain your reasoning. You want to show that you're a critical thinker and a team player who respects the chain of command.

Answer prompts

- *Use your CAR story S27.1 in section 1.4.2.6 (C27-Compliance).*

- *I can't think of a time when that happened. If there is such a time, I believe it is part of my job to point out potential issues before they become problems so I might ask questions or express my concerns, but I would respect the decision and outcome made by my superiors.*

Would you lie for the company?

The hiring manager wants to know if you would choose to be dishonest on the job. It is about your honesty and integrity.

Answer prompts

I believe there is always an honourable way to succeed and always work towards that. I would do what is best for the organization in accordance with company

4. PREPARING FOR AN INTERVIEW

and legal guidelines. I will use my skills in _____, _____, and _____ to resolve any issues that may arise.

4.6.3.6 Learning and growing

Tell me about a time you did something wrong. How did you handle it? • What was your biggest/greatest failure?

The hiring manager wants to know that you can deal with criticism calmly and professionally. Talk about a time when someone told you how you could do something different or better, how you incorporated their advice, and then what the results were.

The best story you could tell is the one where you can demonstrate your skills and strengths in addition to the problem and weaknesses. For example, you can show that you have the courage to admit a mistake, took time to listen to the advice, and followed a plan to solve the problem or overcome a weakness.

You need to show that you've failed, learned from your failure, and corrected the problem going forward. Employers want to find out how you deal with adversity. They are always looking for someone who is not afraid to admit he/she made a mistake, takes responsibility, and is interested in improving himself/herself.

Choose something that would not directly affect your performance at this job.

Answer prompts

- *One time I was/had _____ (problem). I (did) _____ and _____ (the result). I learned from the experience that _____. Ever since, I (do/practise) _____. Now I am proud/glad that I am better at _____.*

- *I used to be _____, which stemmed from my focus on delivering outstanding results. I still am focusing on consistently delivering those results, but I have learned _____, _____, and _____ so everything has worked out very well.*

How did you deal with the situation the last time your manager reprimanded you or disagreed with a statement, a plan, or a decision you made?

Provide a generic answer or describe how you learned from this one-time experience.

Answer prompts

- *I don't have a good example of a time that my manager strongly disagreed with something I did. I believe open communication helps prevent disagreements. I would find out if there are any misunderstandings first. If not and indeed I make a mistake, I would correct it and take steps to not make the same mistake again.*

- *I realized I had made a mistake because _____ (didn't have all the information, there was a misunderstanding…). I've learned from that incident and I am now better at _____. To make sure that doesn't happen again, I _____.*

What is your biggest/greatest regret and why?

Provide a philosophical answer or frame your answer in a positive way if you had issues in the past.

Answer prompts

- *I regret doing _____ instead of _____ as it didn't turn out to be a great move for me. It was the best decision I could have made at the time with the information I had and even though I learned a lot from it, I would change it if I could go back.*

- *I think we all have moments that we wish we go back to do things differently, but overall, I'm pleased with the direction I've taken and the*

> *decisions I've made in my career and in my personal life.*

4.6.3.7 Motivations

What motivates you? • What is your mission statement? • What are your (lifelong) dreams?

Employers want to know what makes you tick and that you are motivated to work harder and better by something besides monetary reward.

Answer prompts

> *I enjoy every aspect of _____ but nothing makes me happier than _____. I love _____ and that's why I'm driven to _____ and _____. I'm highly motivated by _____. In my previous job, I _____ which helped me achieved _____.*

What excites you and scares you about this position?

When the hiring manager asks what excites you and scares you about the position, he/she wants to see if you will tell about any issues or problems you might have while assessing your enthusiasm and approach to the job.

Answer prompts

I'm excited about the opportunity to exceed your expectations and the potential growth once I do that. I know that I can impact _____, _____, and _____ (outcomes the company wants) because I've done it (or something similar) before. I can't say that I'm at all scared about this job, but if I must pick something about being scared, I'd say that the only things that scare me are things that might come up that could delay my success or make it more difficult to attain. But I am not worried though because if it did, I would find a solution.

How long would you plan to stay with us?

The question is not about your long-term plan or career goals. Employers want to eliminate their doubt that you would take off after a short period of time.

Answer prompts

- *I stayed at my last job for _____ years so I plan to stay as long as I can at this job.*

- *I would never have left my previous job if there wasn't a layoff.*

If you won a lottery, would you still work?

The hiring manager wants to find your motivation as to why you are working: for money or because you enjoy the job. He/she wants to understand what will keep you at the job, and how long you would stay if they should hire you. State that you will not be quitting work then talk about what motivated you to get into this type of work and bring up goals that aren't related to money.

Answer prompts

If I won a lottery, I would still work because _____ is something I am passionate about and believe in. I may not put in as many hours, but I love working because it (gives me purpose/it's my calling/this job is who I am). I would have a hard time if I am not able to use all the experiences and skills I've developed, and I would want to use them as long as I can.

What did you dislike about your previous/current job? • What did you like least about your last job?

Discuss aspects of your old job that frustrated you but will be less likely to exist in the position you are applying for. For example, maybe part of this new job is diving into the data that drives the company while at your previous job you had no access to information about what was happening behind the scenes.

Make sure you understand the role and choose things that are not the central pieces of this job's responsibility. Or, provide common answers that anyone would choose such as delivering bad news or failing.

Answer prompts

I dislike dealing with _____ even though I know that they can be helpful so I do everything I can to _____. I enjoy the feeling that I get when I am able to _____. I don't enjoy some of the tasks like _____ and _____ but they are part of my responsibilities so I've implemented _____, _____, and _____ to make them more efficient and pleasant to do. I believe this job is better for me because _____. That's why I'm so looking forward to being able to _____ and _____ here.

4.6.3.8 Work values

What is your best/favourite memory from childhood?

The hiring manager wants to know what kind of person you are and what matters to you. Your answer should speak to your work-related integrity, character, and ethics. Your values should also align with the organization's core values.

Answer prompts

One of my best/favourite childhood memories was _____. That experience may seem small but it taught me the value of _____ which has shaped me into who I am today. I believe such value aligns with the company's core value of _____.

How do you evaluate success?

The hiring manager is interested in what qualities will allow you to succeed. They want to be confident that you are self-motivated and dedicated to your work.

Depending on the role of the job you are applying for, success is based on achieving objectives and satisfying the people who are paying you for work. Talk about successes in customer satisfaction, increasing revenue, gaining more customers, and improving accuracy.

Answer prompts

Success for me means _____, _____, and _____. I will not consider myself successful unless I met all of my own personal requirements and I'm always trying to push them higher and higher and I welcome opportunities to improve.

4.7   Other questions

4.7.1   Salary

Employers want to make sure they can afford you. As most jobs have a pay range, do your homework to find out what the expected salary range of the role is, and then aim for the highest part of that range that applies based on your skills, experience, and education. Knowing the reasonable pay range helps you negotiate after you receive the job offer.

Avoid talking about money for as long as you can. It will be easier to negotiate salary after you convince the employer that you are the perfect candidate for the job.

Answer prompts

- *I've done some research and I understand that the going rate for this job falls somewhere between _____ and _____ dollars. Is that the range you are offering?*

- *What is the salary range you're offering for this position?*

- *I don't think my current (or past) salary is relevant because it was for a different position. I am sure if we can agree that I'm the right person for the job, we'll be able to come to an agreement on compensation.*

- *I am excited about the possibility of working here and if I'm offered a salary within _____ range, I won't turn the offer down because of the money.*

- *That's a great question. We haven't discussed what the salary for this position is. Can you fill me in on that?*

- *I am interested in learning more to see if we're a good fit before we start talking about the money.*

- *I'd like to make _____ amount of money in the next _____ to _____ years. What would you need to see from me to get there? And do you think that goal is attainable?*

4.7.2   Questions for the interviewer

Always say yes when you are asked if you have any questions. Asking questions shows that you are intelligent, excited, and interested. This is also your opportunity to ask questions that can help you decide whether the job is the right fit for you. What do you want to know about the position, the company, the team, the interviewer? Ask questions such as:

- Why is the position open?

- How would you describe the company's culture?

- How would you describe the company's values around work-life balance?

- How would you score the company on living up to its core values?

- What do you think are the current strategic challenges facing the company?

- What's the one thing you're working to improve on?

- What's your staff turnover rate and what are you doing to reduce it?

- What makes people stay at this company?

- If you were to hire me, what might I expect in a typical day?

- What will it take to be successful in this position?

- What type of employee tends to succeed here?

- What qualities are the most important for doing well and advancing at the company?

- Beyond the technical skills required to successfully perform this job, what soft skills would serve the company and position best?

- How do you evaluate success here?

- How does this role fit as part of the whole of the company?

- What have past employees done to succeed in this position?

- What are the three most important challenges for this position?

- What are the long-term expectations for this position?

- Where did the person who was in this role before go?

- When do you want to have the position filled?

- How has this position evolved?

- What would you have me start on when I get here?

- If hired, what are the three most important things you'd like me to accomplish in the first six to 12 months?

- What advice would you give to someone in this role?

- Who would I be reporting to?

- Can you give me an example of how I would collaborate with my manager?

- What's the best thing about working here?

- What do you find most impressive about the company?

- How long have you been at the company?

- Why do you like working here?

- What was your career plan before you got into this role, and how has that changed since you've been here?

- Where do you see yourself in five years? (Ask this question only if they didn't ask you already).

- What's one of the most interesting projects or opportunities that you've worked on?

- How do you respond when your staff comes to you with conflicts?

Or ask about things you learned during your research like new projects, products, initiatives, or strategies the company is pursuing. You can also ask these questions at the appropriate times during the interview as part of a conversation.

Avoid asking the following questions:

- Do you do background checks?

- What are the grounds for termination?

- Can I make personal calls during the day?

- Do you monitor emails or internet usage?

- How soon can I take a vacation?

- Will I have my own office, expense account, car...?

- Will I have to work long hours?

- When will I be eligible for a raise?

- Can I arrive early or leave late as long as I get my work done?

- How quickly could I be considered for a promotion?

- Who should I avoid in the office?

- What happens if I don't get along with my manager or coworkers?

- Are you married?

- Do you have kids?

- Do you check social media accounts?

The interviewers may wait until the end of the interview to ask if you have questions for them. In that situation, some of these general questions might also be helpful:

- Have I answered all your questions?

- Who do you think would be the ideal candidate for this position, and how do I compare?

- Can you tell me what steps need to be completed before your company can generate an offer?

- What's your timeline for making a decision, and when can I expect to hear back from you?

- Is there anything else I can provide to help you make your decision?

4.8   Checklist: Interview

Use this checklist of things to consider when attending an interview:

- ☐ I know as much as possible about the company.

- ☐ I make sure to arrive at the location 10 to 15 minutes before my interview for an on-location interview.

☐ I make sure all equipment is in working order for a remote interview.

☐ I bring a computer, watch, notepad, pen, extra copies of résumé, presentation, references), and my portfolio (optional).

☐ I have a list of questions to ask the interviewers (see section 4.7.2).

☐ I pay close attention to my personal appearance.

☐ I ask for guidance if I am uncertain about how to dress for my interview.

☐ I refrain from using perfume, cologne, or heavy makeup.

☐ I display self-confidence and an appropriate sense of humour.

☐ I treat everyone I meet with respect and consideration.

☐ I show interest and enthusiasm.

☐ I understand the job.

☐ I engage the interviewers.

☐ I speak up and do not speak too fast.

☐ I use examples where appropriate to create vivid images, even for non-behavioural questions.

☐ I substantiate my claims with verifiable results without exaggerating my experience or education.

☐ I assume that the interviewers don't know my experience so I make every response thorough.

☐ When there is more than one interviewer, I give equal eye contact to all panel members throughout the course of the interview.

☐ I write down or remember keywords of questions in order to stay focused on the answers.

☐ I ask for clarification if I don't understand the question.

☐ I listen carefully to questions and take time to think about my responses.

☐ I frame negative experiences or weaknesses as positive lessons learned wherever possible.

☐ I speak positively about myself, my manager, colleagues and organizations I've worked for.

☐ I tell the interviewer if I really don't know the answer as I may be able to come back to it later.

☐ I provide thoughtful feedback or explanations when I disagree with the interviewer.

☐ I ask thoughtful and relevant questions that demonstrate my knowledge of the subject and uncover more information about the organization.

☐ I don't try to fill pauses when the interviewer takes time to read or write.

☐ If I feel that I am rambling, I stop talking and ask a question such as "Does that make sense?" or "What else can I share?"

☐ Right after my interview, I send personalized thank you notes to my interviewer(s) to show that I appreciate their time. I also take this opportunity to expand on answers or to provide a link to a topic discussed.

☐ I post intelligent information about my industry or the economy on my social media networks within 12 hours of the interview.

☐ I follow up with the interviewer(s) at least a week later to show my eagerness.

4.9   Lessons learned

Sometimes you can be the best and still not get selected. If you view this as a rejection, you will feel discouraged. Instead, believe that your value does not diminish because someone fails to see your worth. Take time to review the whole experience. Ask yourself the following questions to assess your performance so you can improve your chance next time:

- What did I do well?

- What didn't I do well?

- What could I improve?

- Have I waited long enough?

- Am I thinking big change but selling incremental?

- Is the jump too big?

- Have I sent enough applications/feelers?

- Did I rush things?

- Am I being direct enough with my network?

- Is this the right time for my target industry?

- Is this the right time in general?

- Did I learn anything?

- What can I bring forward with me?

- Am I focused on the results of today, or at the finish line?

If possible, ask the interviewer who may be willing to give you some feedback. The direct feedback can be uncomfortable but helpful because it may teach you how to present yourself next time, or what skills or experience you need to be successful in the future.

5 GETTING A JOB OFFER

5.1 Accepting a job offer

It's a great feeling to receive a job offer, especially after a long, anxious search. You may feel relieved, excited, or validated that another employer has recognized that you've got the right stuff and is willing to invest in you.

Re-read the first chapter of this book to see if the job gives you all the things you wanted and whether the move is right for you.

In addition, use this checklist to evaluate the job offer to see whether it makes financial sense for you to accept it.

5.1.1 Checklist: Evaluating the job offer

☐ Will I gain/lose any salary, bonus, or benefits/perks?

- ☐ Will I gain/lose any equity on my property?

- ☐ Will I gain/lose any stock options or other investments?

- ☐ Will I incur moving expenses?

- ☐ How do the costs of living compare?

- ☐ How do the rent/mortgage payments compare?

- ☐ How do income, sales, and other taxes compare?

- ☐ How do the auto, house, and other insurance policies and rates compare?

- ☐ How do transportation times and costs compare?

- ☐ How do public/private schools or daycare quality and arrangements compare?

- ☐ How do public/private schools or daycare costs compare?

Negotiate before accepting a job offer. Be clear, realistic, and flexible. Negotiate only the most important things because the organization can reject your requests and may judge you for the things you're asking for. Negotiate salary first if it is important to you.

5.1.2   Checklist: Things I want to negotiate

☐ Salary

☐ Benefits/perks

☐ Relocation costs

☐ Job title

☐ Job description

☐ Training and conferences costs

☐ Professional dues

☐ Start date

☐ Working hours

☐ Vacation

☐ Work-from-home days

☐ Bonuses

☐ Stock options/programs

☐ Profit sharing

☐ Insurance

☐ Pension

☐ Expenses

☐ Parking spot

☐ Office

☐ Tools /equipment

☐ _____

After you've finished negotiating the job offer, ask for some time to consider it because taking a job you're unhappy with can end badly, and it's harder to look for another job once you've started this new one.

After you've accepted the job offer, you will need to give your current employer notice that you are leaving. The notice is usually two weeks and in writing but find out what it is required where you are and be aware of common practices in your industry. Always leave on good terms because you may later encounter a co-worker again or need to call the company for information or a favour.

5.2 Declining a job offer

Turning down a reasonable job offer shouldn't be done lightly. Ask for a day or two to think it over once the final offer is on the table. Consider declining the job offer if the job does not fulfill your needs and wants, if you have any doubts, or if your gut is telling you something you don't want to hear.

Regardless of why you choose to turn down a job offer, there are ways of doing so that don't slam the door shut for later.

Let the employer know as soon as you've made your decision, so that you don't keep them waiting unnecessarily. Speak directly to the person who made you the offer. Be brief, upbeat, and say something like, "Thank you for the opportunity to discuss the job with you and everything you've done for me. I believe this place is a great place to work but after taking everything into account, I've decided to continue my search (or stay where I am) at this time. I'd love to have a chance to come back when my circumstances change."

6   REFERENCES & TOOLS

6.1   100 Action power words

Accelerated	Designed	Increased	Presented
Advanced	Detected	Influenced	Programmed
Announced	Developed	Initiated	Projected
Appraised	Discovered	Innovated	Promoted
Assessed	Eliminated	Instituted	Provided
Assigned	Enhanced	Integrated	Qualified
Attained	Enriched	Invented	Quantified
Attracted	Established	Investigated	Quoted
Balanced	Exceeded	Justified	Recommended
Bargained	Excelled	Launched	Recovered
Bolstered	Financed	Led	Reduced
Boosted	Fixed	Listed	Refined
Built	Forecasted	Logged	Reinstated
Closed	Formulated	Maintained	Retained
Collaborated	Fulfilled	Managed	Revamped
Completed	Generated	Measured	Saved
Complied	Granted	Mentored	Scheduled
Created	Guided	Multiplied	Screened
Critiqued	Helped	Negotiated	Secured
Cut	Hosted	Observed	Segmented
Delegated	Implemented	Obtained	Simplified
Demonstrated	Improved	Operated	Sold

Solved	Supported	Trained	Updated
Streamlined	Sustained	Unified	Upgraded
Strengthened	Taught	United	Validated

6.2   Phrases to avoid

Avoid these wordy phrases to make your writing clean, crisp, and easier to read:

Above-mentioned	In this connection
Aforementioned	In this day and age
As a matter of fact	It goes without saying
As I am sure you know	It is interesting to note that
As the case may be	It is my belief that
As you know	Kind of/sort of
At hand	Last but not least
Beg to advise/differ/state	Let me add that
Be that as it may	Literally and figuratively
For all intents and purposes	Needless to say
Give this matter your attention	Not to mention
I have ascertained that	Permit me to say
In all honesty	To tell the truth
In connection with	When/after all is said and done
In the case of	With all due regard
In the final analysis	Words cannot describe

6.3   Useful links

- Organize & Manage Your Job Search
  https://www.jibberjobber.com

- SHL https://www.shldirect.com — Free career planning tool and skills certifications tests available in several languages.

- Top 500 Résumé Keywords to Boost Your Résumé https://www.jobscan.co/blog/top-resume-keywords-boost-resume.

- 30-60-90 Plan https://blog.hubspot.com/marketing/30-60-90-day-plan — How to write a 30-60-90 plan for an interview.

- Technical Interview Questions and Answers https://www.careerride.com/Technical-Interview-Questions.aspx

- Glassdoor's Know Your Worth https://www.glassdoor.com/Salaries/know-your-worth.htm — Free and personalized salary estimate based on your title, company, location and experience.

- Salary.com's What are you worth? https://www.salary.com/salaries — Free salary reports covering U.S. and Canadian markets.

6.4 Downloadable resources

Visit http://www.because.zone/join-us/bmm3-reg/ and create an account to gain free access to the worksheets, templates, and checklists in this book.

MAY YOU FIND YOUR NEXT BETTER JOB

Thank you for the opportunity to share my knowledge and experiences with you. I hope you've gained something from this book.

Think of yourself as the CEO of your career. This helps remind you that you have full control in planning and achieving your career goals. You are responsible for building, maintaining, and fixing your career as needed. Your chances of success increase when you see yourself as someone who has something to offer a prospective employer instead of as an applicant looking and hoping for a job. When you see your qualifications as facts without emotional investment, you'll gain different perspectives and more opportunities.

Reading alone will not get you what you want but working smarter will. Keep learning and experimenting. You will get better with practice.

I'd love to hear your story of how this book has helped you with your career. That would be the best feedback I could hope for! I would also appreciate it if you'd post a short review for this book. Your review is an invaluable tool to let other readers know what to expect and help them decide whether this book would be useful to them. It will help me to make continuous improvements based on your comments and suggestions as well. Would you please take a few seconds to let your social networking friends know about this book if you think they would benefit from it? Thank you.

Please feel free to reach out to me at vvcam@because.zone if I can be of further assistance to you in any way.

Blessings to you and I wish you find your next better job as you wish!

V.

ACKNOWLEDGEMENTS

To my daughter, Candace, thank you for being the best daughter any mother can hope for. You are my biggest accomplishment and best gift.

To the Quiethouse Editing team of beta readers, Bridgit Davis and Jesse Savage, thank you for your invaluable feedback. I appreciate your respectful comments and considerate suggestions. Thank you again, Starr Waddell, for another pleasant experience with your professional and friendly service.

To my amazing editor, David Loving from davidaloving.com, thank you for your care and competence.

To all my supporters, thank you for your consistent motivation and support throughout my writing process.

Thank you to my husband, Jack, for always being here and now. With you in my life, each day is better than the last.

ABOUT THE AUTHOR

V.V. and her family had to flee Vietnam by boat when she was just at the tender age of 13. When most young girls at that age would have been worrying about acne and boys, she was living in Hong Kong, housed in a prison that had been turned into an overcrowded refugee camp.

That was where she started her journey to become the happy and successful wife, mother, and entrepreneur that she is today. While working in an electronics factory earning money to help her family survive the hardships of daily life, she taught herself to read and write Chinese. A year later, a church sponsored her family to start their new life in a small town in Ontario, Canada.

She put her language learning skills to use again, this time mastering English. She soon became one of the top students at her school and helped the office staff with her typing and office skills. Along with her industrious family, she learned to sew and made money sewing for local shops and for friends.

Her résumé soon included an impressive list of accomplishments: She worked her way from seamstress, waitress, bartender, and receptionist to IT support specialist and trainer, to real estate agent and broker. She has worked in executive positions with large organizations managing finances, human resources, and relationships and has built a couple of small businesses.

In her spare time, she created two high-traffic and successful websites that offer teaching tools and support to the Vietnamese communities. She's also founded a philanthropic organization that provides micro loans for poor people in Vietnam.

V. V. Cam's published books in the *Because Self-Publishing Works* series share the knowledge she learned while helping her husband publish and market his book. This book is the third in the *Because Money Matters* series. Find out more about her books at http://www.because.zone/books-by-v-v-cam.

You will appreciate her usual pragmatic advice, compassionate voice, and succinct writing style.

V. V. Cam lives in Toronto, Canada with her family.

BOOKS BY V.V. CAM

http://www.because.zone/books-by-v-v-cam

Because Self-Publishing Works Series:

Book 1 – Everything I Learned About How to Publish a Book

Book 2 – Everything I Learned About How to Market a Book

The two books in the Because Self-Publishing Works series

(http://www.because.zone/because-self-publishing-works) share the knowledge

V. V. Cam learned while helping her husband publish and market his book,

because *– a novel by Jack A. Langedijk (http://www.because.zone).*

Because Money Matters Series:

Book 1 – The 8 Principles to Build Your Wealth

Book 2 – How to Earn More Money as a Freelancer

in a Gig Economy

Book 3 – How to Find and Get a Better Job

INDEX

NOTES

NOTES

NOTES

NOTES